Records and Information Management Core Competencies, 2nd Ed.

ARMA
INTERNATIONAL®

Overland Park, KS

Cover Art: Brett Dietrich

ARMA International
11880 College Blvd., Suite 450
Overland Park, KS 66210
913.341.3808

ISBN: 978-1-936654-78-9

A5034 (PDF version)

Table of Contents

Foreword

Records and information management (RIM) professionals at all stages of their career can use *Records and Information Management Core Competencies, 2nd Ed.* to identify their proficiency in each of six defined domains: Business Functions, RIM/Information Governance Practices, Risk Management, Communications and Marketing, Information Technology, and Leadership.

This publication, which supersedes 2007's first edition, has been updated to reflect the elevated skills RIM professionals need to 1) meet significantly more challenging technology issues; and 2) assume a more proactive and collaborative role to ensure a strong RIM foundation for their organization's information governance program.

By defining the knowledge and skills needed to perform successfully in the profession, ARMA International demonstrates its ongoing commitment to define and develop the RIM profession.

This material was developed under procedures designed to ensure a large, balanced representation of contributors and reviewers at all levels of expertise, in all domains, and from a variety of industries. Although the procedures ensure the highest degree of care, ARMA, its members, and those participating in its activities do not accept any liability resulting from compliance or noncompliance with the provisions given herein, for any restrictions imposed on materials or processes, or for the completeness of the text. ARMA has no power or authority to police or enforce compliance with the contents of this document. Any certification or product stating compliance with requirements of this document is made at the peril of the certifier.

Comments on the content of this publication should be sent by e-mail to *education@armaintl.org* or by mail to:

> ARMA International
> Executive Director of Content and Programming
> 11880 College Blvd., Suite 450
> Overland Park, KS 66210

Acknowledgments

The second edition of the *Records and Information Management Core Competencies* was developed through a year-long process that included the input of the 32 records management and information governance professionals named below, who reviewed, edited, and commented on the original 2007 core competencies and wrote additional competencies. Afterward, 163 subject matter experts participated in a validation survey, reviewing the work and providing additional comments and recommendations.

ARMA International gratefully acknowledges their contributions.

Second Edition Group Members

Vera Beck, Legislative Assembly of Alberta

Alexandra Bradley, CRM, FAI, Harwood Information Associates Limited

Diane K. Carlisle, IGP, CRM
ARMA International

Raymond K. Cunningham, Jr., CRM, CA, CDIA+, CIP, CIPP, University of Illinois Foundation

Lorrie DeCoursey, RICOH USA, Inc.

Michael DeVanna, CRM, Aramco Services Company

Sandra Dunkin, IGP, CRM, First Nations Summit Society

Nicholas Fonseca, CIP, ARMA Canada

Uta Fox, CRM, Calgary Police Service

Kristina Franz, ARMA International

Glenn Gercken, CRM, Nixon Peabody LLP

Michele Havens, Navantis, Inc.

Margaret Hermesmeyer, IGP, CRM, Office of Attorney General of Texas

Leigh Isaacs, IGP, CIP, White & Case LLP

Tao Jin, Louisiana State University

Mary Laverdure, CRM, Wells Fargo

William LeFevre, CRM, CA, Wayne State University

Scott McVeigh, Deloitte Transactions and Business Analytics LLP

Carolyn Offutt, IGP, CRM, CIP, PMP, Offutt Advisory Services LLC

Linda Pace, Prudential Financial

Jennifer Ransom, City of Murrieta

Stuart Rennie, Esq.

Shuntrela Rogers-Gillion, Georgia Power Environmental Affairs

Theresa Sippert, CIPP, Canadian Blood Services

Raymond Soh, EnQuest Malaysia

Amitabh Srivastav, PMP, Canada Deposit Insurance Corporation

Courtney Stone, IGP, CRM, AMOCO Federal Credit Union

Helen Streck, Kaizen InfoSource LLC

Cheryl Strom, McDonald's Corporation

Melissa Suek, IGP, CRM, Pricewaterhouse Coopers LLP

Todd Varel, CRM, The iQ Business Group

Andrew Ysasi, IGP, CRM, CIPP, PMP, Kent Record Management

ARMA International also would like to acknowledge the process of the original RIM core competencies, which were developed in 2006-2007 and the many individuals who contributed to that effort. This information can be found on page 112.

Introduction

Purpose and Scope

The records and information management (RIM) core competencies are a useful resource for RIM practitioners and others, such as human resource professionals, IT peers and partners, executive-level managers, policy-makers, product developers, vendors, educational institutions, and certifying entities.

While the core competencies may complement the course of study for various certification exams, this document should not be construed as a single study aid for any exam; it is intended to be a resource for a much wider audience.

What Are Competencies?

Competencies are defined as the knowledge, skills, characteristics, or traits that contribute to outstanding performance in a particular profession. They are described in a way that makes them observable, measurable, and rate-able. Competencies move the focus from "what" an employee must accomplish (defined in the typical job description) to "how" the employee accomplishes the required tasks.

When series of competencies are organized, the result is called a competency model. A competency model differentiates between entry-level and expert-level performance for a specific profession. Competencies create a common bond of understanding and a common language for discussing performance requirements. They also may be used to design and develop training and educational programs, position descriptions, and performance evaluation instruments.

Why Evaluate One's Competencies?

Organizations using competency-based programs will realize benefits in:

- Hiring
- Establishing performance expectations
- Providing employee feedback
- Managing employees
- Training and development
- Guiding career development
- Making succession plans

Individuals using competencies will realize benefits in:

- Identifying gaps between their current knowledge and skill sets and those required to advance to the next job level
- Having points to discuss with their supervisors regarding their job performance, career aspirations, and development needs
- Creating professional development plans to help them excel in their position, organization, and profession
- Identifying educational resources to address their areas of professional need

Organization of the Core Competencies

The core competencies are organized by competency level and performance domain:

- **Levels:** Reflect the amount of knowledge or experience a person has relative to a specific topic or skill set, regardless of time in the profession. The competencies are divided into four levels and are intended to represent a progression of responsibilities from the entry-level practitioner to the executive-level professional.
- **Domains:** Groups or categories of competencies in a particular performance area that are the major responsibilities or duties of the profession. There are six domains in these RIM core competencies: Business Functions, RIM/Information Governance Practices, Risk Management, Communications and Marketing, Information Technology, and Leadership.

The core competencies are organized by competency level and domain. Within each domain are task statements. Following each task are statements identifying the knowledge and skills required to perform the task competently.

The four levels are outlined hierarchically. The design is intended to acknowledge how knowledge and skill sets increase from entry-level to executive-level positions. In contrast, the task statements within the levels and domains *are not* ordered by their significance or importance.

Some instances of the knowledge and skills may appear in many tasks. For example, effective communication skills are necessary for reporting, mentoring, and advocating within all domains and levels.

The developers purposely chose not to insert specific job titles into the discussion because the scope of the levels and position titles will vary among organizations. Because knowledge and skill requirements will vary as well, the competencies should not be used as job descriptions. However, components of the competencies can be used to create organization-specific job descriptions. (ARMA International's *Job Descriptions for Records and Information Management,* which is available for purchase at _www.arma.org/bookstore_, provides sample job descriptions in electronic templates that can be customized to fit any organization.)

Realistically, an individual may not demonstrate all the knowledge and skills at one level before progressing to the next. The organization's structure and goals should be considered when determining if a knowledge or skill is relevant.

These core competencies include the leading-edge RIM knowledge and skills required within a domain and level, as well as the knowledge and skills from related areas such as IT and general management. Each progressive level assumes competence in the levels before it within the domain.

Competency Levels

The competencies are divided into four levels:

Level 1: The level 1 practitioners hold an entry-level position in the RIM profession, a position requiring no previous RIM experience. They should be acquiring foundational knowledge and skills for the RIM field; have a basic understanding of what RIM encompasses; understand the importance of information privacy and security; and be familiar with general business functions outside of the RIM function, such as accounting and human resources. Individuals at this level may have an undergraduate degree or work experience in another field.

Level 2: The level 2 practitioners will have prior RIM knowledge, skills, and experience. They understand more than the basic techniques and technologies; have managed or developed RIM projects; have knowledge of information management lifecycle concepts; and understand how privacy and security should be integrated in a RIM program. They may be developing specialty skills (e.g., analysis, auditing, warehousing, and using technologies) and may have experience supervising other RIM staff. They understand how different areas of the business work together and how the organization views its RIM practices. Practitioners at this level generally hold an undergraduate degree, usually in a RIM-related field; if not, they generally have lower level RIM experience.

Level 3: This level is composed of seasoned practitioners who have worked at the enterprise level and have extensive knowledge of the design, creation, implementation, and management of a RIM program. They have applied information privacy and security practices and look to high-level experts for additional best practices, advanced techniques, and technology innovations to learn more and advance in the field. They engage across the organization to improve RIM practices and procedures. Practitioners at this level may hold advanced degrees and generally have earned appropriate professional certifications.

Level 4: These executive-level professionals make strategic decisions, partner with other executives, and give enterprise direction to RIM program staff and program users. They champion the way the RIM program supports the goals and strategy of the organization, and they influence others to champion the RIM program. They help ensure that there are strategic measures to integrate and sustain information privacy and security throughout the organization and that litigation and regulatory obligations are met through established RIM practices. They frequently hold advanced degrees and appropriate certifications. Their continuing education focuses on business strategy, change management, business policies, leading teams, and collaborations and partnerships.

Assumptions

The RIM core competencies were developed with the following assumptions about business operational skills.

It is assumed that practitioners at Level 1 can demonstrate:

1. Basic computational skills
2. Basic, legible writing skills
3. Basic keyboarding skills
4. Reading comprehension
5. The ability to follow directions and procedures
6. Familiarity with RIM and information governance (IG) terms

It is assumed that practitioners at Level 2 should be able to:

1. Apply percentages and ratios to numerical data that may be collected
2. Compare growth and decreases in numerical data between defined periods of time
3. Respond in writing to requests for information
4. Demonstrate advanced keyboarding and data entry skills
5. Demonstrate basic skills with Office suite products, RIM software applications, and databases
6. Conduct simple, efficient information searches successfully
7. Demonstrate basic project management skills
8. Understand concepts and best practices that support the RIM department
9. Understand the importance of IG principles and practices to a RIM program

It is assumed that practitioners at Level 3 should be able to:

1. Develop, submit, and adjust a budget and monitor expenditures
2. Convert numerical data into chart and graph formats
3. Demonstrate problem-solving techniques
4. Perform research and present results in an appropriate format (chart, report, narrative)
5. Demonstrate proficiency with Office suite products, RIM software applications, and databases
6. Conduct complex, efficient information searches successfully
7. Implement and audit RIM systems
8. Integrate IG requirements (e.g., information security, privacy, litigation response, and audit principles) with RIM program execution

It is assumed that practitioners at Level 4 should be able to:

1. Conduct surveys and validate analysis and results
2. Interpret complex data and evaluate independent studies and results
3. Use data sets to perform and analyze research
4. Use language and vocabulary appropriately, including professional terminology and jargon
5. Make presentations to and engage in meaningful discussion with peers and business professionals regarding information-related goals, challenges, and solutions
6. Propose optimal RIM/IG systems
7. Develop and lead RIM/IG program strategy and advocacy
8. Review, audit, benchmark, and measure RIM program success
9. Research new concepts, technologies, and business functions that support the RIM program
10. Collaborate with other IG stakeholders to develop and lead IG initiatives

Domains

The core competencies are organized within each level by domains (groups or categories of competencies in a particular performance area), which define the major responsibilities or duties within the profession. Each competency level contains elements of each domain.

The six competency domains are:

- **Business Functions:** This domain pertains to the knowledge and skills necessary to administer, implement, or maintain the non-RIM-specific functions an organization performs, or needs to perform, to achieve its objectives. Examples of business functions include supervising RIM staff, budgeting, providing customer service, identifying and mapping work processes, auditing, working in cross-functional groups, providing input to management, and performing strategic planning.

- **RIM/IG Practices:** This domain pertains to the knowledge and skills required to systematically manage information assets from creation or receipt through processing, distributing, sharing, using, accessing, organizing, storing and retrieving, and disposing of them. Information is a vital organizational asset, and organizations depend on accurate, complete, and readily available information to assist in decision-making; providing litigation support; improving organizational efficiency; documenting compliance with legislative, regulatory, contractual, and audit requirements; and providing historical reference.

- **Risk Management:** This domain pertains to the knowledge and skills necessary to proactively mitigate and manage the potential for damage, loss, or unauthorized access to information assets. Two risk management components—risk analysis, which identifies the probabilities that information will be damaged or lost, and risk assessment, which examines known or anticipated risk to information—are key concepts to systematically controlling the level of risk exposure of an organization. Additional risk management components from an operational perspective are business continuity, disaster preparedness and recovery, information privacy and security requirements, and auditing.

- **Communications and Marketing:** This domain pertains to the knowledge and skills necessary to effectively exchange thoughts, messages, or information by speech, writing, or behavior and to effectively champion the benefits of a RIM program within an organization or to external stakeholders. The domain covers training and educating users about the RIM program. The Communications and Marketing domain is vital to developing successful business relationships to maximize RIM support and compliance, communicate the importance of RIM, and promote the value of RIM principles and best practices.

- **Information Technology:** This domain pertains to the knowledge and skills necessary to develop, maintain, and use information processing systems, software applications, and supporting hardware and networks used for processing data, distributing data, and protecting electronic and physical information assets at all times and in any state. Examples of IT tasks in this context include selecting RIM software applications; establishing requirements for IT related to managing databases, collaboration sites, and mobile applications; ensuring information security controls are in place and operational; and identifying emerging technologies. Because RIM operates in an electronic and digital environment, a solid understanding of the technological impact on RIM requirements and solutions is essential. For a RIM professional, this includes knowledge and skills in relevant aspects of IT at all competency levels.

- **Leadership:** This domain pertains to the knowledge and skills necessary to increase RIM awareness and motivate groups of people toward the achievement of the RIM program goals within the context of the organization's overall goals. Effective leaders must positively influence others by using leadership skills such as guiding, motivating, mentoring, and promoting continuing education and learning; interpersonal skills such as empathy and sensitivity; creative thinking skills such as brainstorming and thinking untraditionally; and change management skills such as trust building and networking.

Tasks, Knowledge, and Skills

Within the core competencies, task statements are defined for each level and domain combination. Each task statement addresses a specific work activity. In general, task statements answer the following questions:

- What activity is performed?
- To whom or at what is the activity directed?
- How is the activity accomplished?
- Why is this activity performed?

Taken together, task statements offer a comprehensive view of the work activities each domain comprises at each level.

Following each task are statements identifying the knowledge and skills required to perform the task competently. *Knowledge statements* are learned factual or procedural information that support the ability to perform the task statement. A *skill* embodies observable, quantifiable, and measurable performance parameters that involve physical, verbal, or mental manipulation of data, people, or objects.

Knowledge and skills are the elements that together demonstrate competency of a specific task statement. Mastery of tasks within a domain and level is needed to advance to the next level of domain specialty. Within a particular organization, mastery in several domains at a level is necessary for advancement to the next level.

How to Use the Competencies for Self-Evaluation

To most effectively use the core competencies for self-evaluation, follow these steps:

1. Identify which of the four levels best reflects your current job responsibilities.
2. Identify which of the six domains are relevant to your current job and organization. More than one domain will likely apply.
3. Review all the task statements at the levels and domains you have identified as matching your current job requirements. Select any tasks within that level/domain combination that are relevant to the performance of your job.
4. For each knowledge and skill statement for the tasks you selected, assess your current level of performance on a pre-defined scale. A suggested scale would be: little or no proficiency, low proficiency, moderate proficiency, high proficiency, or complete proficiency.
5. For all items where you rate yourself as having little or no proficiency or low proficiency, identify methods for improving that knowledge or skill. Such methods could include formal education, training programs or courses, on-the-job training, mentoring, or specific job assignments that allow you to grow or stretch your skills. You may want to consult with your supervisor, with colleagues at the same or advanced levels, or with your human resource or training departments, or use resources from professional organizations such as ARMA International.
6. Consolidate the identified improvement methods into a professional development plan with specific goals and timelines. Review your plan with your supervisor and solicit his or her help in providing opportunities for on-the-job training and "stretch" assignments, as well as support for appropriate training.
7. Reassess your competency level at least once a year and update your personal development plan. You should be able to use your assessment to demonstrate continuous performance improvement to your supervisor. Completion of certain training programs or demonstrated job experience could qualify you for professional certifications.

Level 1: Practitioners at this level hold an entry-level position in the RIM profession, a position requiring no previous RIM experience. They should be acquiring foundational knowledge and skills for the RIM field; have a basic understanding of what RIM encompasses; understand the importance of information privacy and security; and be familiar with general business functions outside of the RIM function, such as accounting and human resources. Individuals at this level may have an undergraduate degree or work experience in another field.

Domain: Business Functions

Business Functions: This domain pertains to the knowledge and skills necessary to administer, implement, or maintain the non-RIM-specific functions an organization performs, or needs to perform, to achieve its objectives. Examples of business functions include supervising RIM staff, budgeting, providing customer service, identifying and mapping work processes, auditing, working in cross-functional groups, providing input to management, and performing strategic planning.

Level 1

Provide input to management about activity levels and program metrics based on current and assigned workload. (010101)

Knowledge of:	*Skills:*
• Organizational and/or departmental policies and procedures	• Identify, compile, sort, organize, and record appropriate data
	• Communicate results and findings effectively, using established formats and reporting tools
	• Basic oral and written communication skills

Identify and provide input to RIM management about ways to improve business processes and therefore improve the RIM program as well. (010102)

Knowledge of:	*Skills:*
• Basic RIM principles	• Understand and effectively communicate RIM workflow processes
• Organizational RIM practices	
• Basic written communication	
• Basic technology used in the organization	

Provide input to management about the need for more effective facility layout to improve information processing and delivery. (010103)

Knowledge of:	*Skills:*
• Basic RIM principles	• Understand and effectively communicate RIM workflow processes
• Organizational RIM practices	• Problem-solving
	• Creative thinking

Inform RIM management of issues within the departments that could affect RIM compliance and program performance. (010104)

Knowledge of:

- Compliance requirements as outlined in organizational policies and procedures
- Internal business customers and stakeholders
- RIM/IG principles and best practices

Skills:

- Effectively communicate with RIM stakeholders, orally and in writing
- Prepare reports using pre-defined formats and data-gathering tools
- Identify errors that could cause compliance or system performance issues
- Identify gaps between current state and compliance state related to RIM processes

Collect data and documentation required to support the management of budget and expenditures. (010105)

Knowledge of:

- Cost-effective work methods
- Organization's budget process
- Applicable software and financial spreadsheets
- Information sources, including cost reports, budget, prior expenditure data

Skills:

- Collect data for budget and input information
- Collect data and documentation for submission according to defined procedures

Process incoming information using appropriate technology and equipment. (010106)

Knowledge of:

- Alpha/numeric filing conventions
- Metadata, taxonomy and tagging conventions for electronic records
- User needs for access and/or distribution
- Security and privacy requirements and deadlines for processing incoming information or requests

Skills:

- Sort information for distribution
- Use available technology for capturing, storing, and retrieving information
- Integrate information to appropriate system locations (e.g., document management, collaborative spaces, enterprise content management system) for access
- Consolidate information for common access and/or delivery points

Manage reference materials, which may include procuring external materials, organizing holdings, and tracking the location of materials. Materials may include standards, technical reports, research papers, and digital resources. (010107)

Knowledge of:

- Basic procurement methodology
- Communications with outside organizations to arrange for purchase or loan
- Inventory management and maintenance procedures for tracking holdings
- Automated tools required to manage, categorize, organize, and arrange repository information assets
- Knowledge of resource description methods

Skills:

- Locate and order reference materials
- Place purchase orders and track their status
- Communicate appropriately for the task, orally and in writing
- Track and monitor holdings in circulation
- Use database/records/repository management systems for inputting and reporting
- Apply barcode, RFID, or other tracking mechanisms

Assist in locating information to support records compliance audits. (010108)

Knowledge of:
- Audit and compliance procedures
- RIM program policy, practices, procedures, and documentation
- Technology and equipment used to manage information assets

Skills:
- Identify and locate the records required to complete a compliance audit

Verify data in the RIM software application according to established procedures. (010109)

Knowledge of:
- Data-input techniques
- Information proofing techniques
- Applicable software
- Authoritative information source or system

Skills:
- Monitor data quality and remediate per organization standards
- Assess, analyze, and correct data in line with RIM program best practices and requirements

Monitor the filing and/or retention of document versions according to organization policy. (010110)

Knowledge of:
- Version-tracking technology and mechanisms
- Policies and organization standards for version management
- Retention policies and management
- Capture and backup processes for version management
- Scanning equipment settings and backup procedures

Skills:
- Capture metadata
- Organize and classify records
- Identify documents that are not appropriately versioned
- Take remedial steps to correct inaccuracies

Domain: RIM/IG Practices

RIM/IG Practices: This domain pertains to the knowledge and skills required to systematically manage information assets from their creation or receipt through processing, distributing, sharing, using, accessing, organizing, storing and retrieving, and disposing of them. Information is a vital organizational asset, and organizations depend on accurate, complete, and readily available information to assist in decision-making; providing litigation support; improving organizational efficiency; documenting compliance with legislative, regulatory, contractual, and audit requirements; and providing historical reference.

Level I

Gather RIM/IG metrics to support project requests and to advance RIM/IG program implementation. (010201)

Knowledge of:

- Enterprise-wide, organizationally used applications
- Content and format of data used in applications
- Information collection methods
- Third-party-owned applications and storage

Skills:

- Identify, compile, sort, organize, and record appropriate data
- Use organizationally supported and third-party-owned systems, applications and tools
- Identify exceptions and flag them
- Report results and findings
- Establish performance levels
- Report progress on goals and performance

Perform basic records center operations in accordance with established RIM/IG procedures. (010202)

Knowledge of:

- Record center operations
- Facility and work safety practices
- Facility security procedures
- Record center equipment and machinery
- Computer programs used for basic records center operations
- Destruction practices for specific media types
- Industry standards and methodologies
- Documentation required to show that legal hold processes have been followed before records are destroyed

Skills:

- Physically carry boxes
- Enter inventory data
- Operate equipment and machinery
- Complete certification for equipment/machinery operation
- Generate reports related to records center activity levels

Demonstrate proficiency in the use of RIM/IG technologies to support the education and training of end users. (010203)

Knowledge of:

- RIM/IG/enterprise content management (ECM) technologies
- Departmental use of RIM/IG/ECM technologies to assist with records retrieval
- Training materials created by the organization

Skills:

- Respond to questions from end users or redirect them to subject matter experts
- Demonstrate proficiency with deployed RIM/IG/ECM technologies
- Communicate appropriately for the task, orally and in writing
- Document training activities

Help review the RIM/IG forms so they are current and consistent with organizational needs. (010204)

Knowledge of:

- Organizational forms management practices
- Use of forms and end-user requirements
- RIM/IG program requirements with respect to forms management
- Electronic forms development and management

Skills:

- Understand the purpose of each form
- Apply the procedure for updating the forms
- Communicate with forms designers (electronic and/or hard copy) regarding end user input
- Notify forms users of changes to obsolete and updated forms

Capture, store, and provide access to documents and records in accordance with organizational policies and procedures. (010205)

Knowledge of:

- Enterprise hardware and software
- Secure access and transmission options
- Documentation styles, templates, and guidelines
- Organizational taxonomy and metadata standards
- Organizational policies and procedures

Skills:

- Identify, compile, and sort data
- Communicate appropriately for the task, orally and in writing
- Understand the workflow processes
- Access and transmit documents and records securely

Classify and process records according to RIM/IG procedures so related records are linked, retrievable, and meet organizational compliance requirements. (010206)

Knowledge of:

- Organizational classification structures, taxonomies, or other controlled language
- Legacy and current systems in which records are managed
- Migration methodologies and strategies specific to the organization's systems
- Organizational structure and functions
- Compliance requirements
- Records retention policy, procedures, and schedules
- Definitions of personally identifiable information (PII), sensitive personally identifiable information (SPII), and protected health information (PHI)
- Conversion techniques for records in electronic format

Skills:

- Think analytically
- Solve problems
- Provide customer service
- Apply practical knowledge of policies, procedures, and systems
- Apply knowledge of PII to its redaction where appropriate
- Apply business regulations to materials being processed
- Organizational enterprise content management or other records systems

Process records involved with mergers, acquisitions, divestitures, and reorganizations by applying classification and taxonomy schemes using established RIM/IG controls and processes. (010207)

Knowledge of:

- Organizational structure
- Records inventory process
- Basic records appraisal principles
- Generally Accepted Recordkeeping Principles® and best practices
- Applicable RIM/enterprise content management software
- Terminologies used in records classification, taxonomies, and schemes
- Basic database management principles and methods

Skills:

- Think analytically
- Organize and analyze collected data
- Solve problems
- Communicate effectively for the task orally and in writing
- Provide customer service
- Resolve conflicting data prior to data entry

Provide assistance in using controlled vocabulary (e.g., thesauri, taxonomies). (010208)

Knowledge of:

- Role and purpose of thesauri in RIM/IG systems
- Organizational RIM/IG program and standards
- Industry and company terminology

Skills:

- Communicate benefits of using controlled vocabulary
- Train end users in use of controlled vocabulary
- Identify and communicate the need for changes to the controlled vocabulary

Perform assigned data entry to populate RIM/IG software according to established procedures. (010209)

Knowledge of:

- Applicable software and how it's used in the organization
- Terminology used in records classification, taxonomies, file schemes, and file-naming conventions
- Scanning requirements

Skills:

- Think analytically
- Enter data accurately
- Resolve conflicting data prior to entry
- Analyze and evaluate data
- Proofread to ensure the accuracy of data, metrics, and reports
- Identify and correct inaccurate entries

Perform imaging, digitizing, and microfilming activities in support of the RIM/IG program following established procedures. (010210)

Knowledge of:

- Imaging software and procedures for consistent metadata capture
- How to operate basic imaging hardware
- Imaging process procedures
- Media for appropriate preparation and set-up
- Quality control procedures for image validation
- Preparation requirements for source documents
- Menu systems used for data capture during entry
- Applicable industry standards for quality

Skills:

- Solve problems
- Manage time and multitask
- Capture information accurately
- Use imaging software and equipment
- Collect information for consistent metadata entry (indexing) to describe images
- Prepare documents properly for "batch" capture
- Verify quality of images during their capture
- Verify all images in a batch are captured
- Communicate effectively with systems staff, orally and in writing
- Redact images in accordance with defined criteria
- Perform basic equipment maintenance tasks
- Verify images are routed to the correct location in the electronic repositories

Perform physical file maintenance tasks, including interfiling and applying tracking or identifying labels to maintain the integrity of the records. (010211)

Knowledge of:

- Filing methods and procedures
- Terminology used in records classifications, taxonomies, file schemes, and file-naming conventions
- Configurations for equipment used in the process
- Lateral filing and color coding

Skills:

- Apply labels
- Operate the equipment used in file maintenance (e.g., mobile file systems)
- Apply business classification standards

Respond to specific requests by searching, locating, retrieving, and delivering information assets through established procedures and delivery systems in a timely manner. (010212)

Knowledge of:

- Taxonomies
- Generally Accepted Recordkeeping Principles® and best practices
- Records retrieval and user service provision principles and practices
- Search techniques
- RIM/IG program policies and procedures
- Organizational requirements for record security, privacy, classification, and access
- Freedom of Information requirements (if applicable)

Skills:

- Locate and retrieve information using physical/manual search skills
- Communicate effectively for the task, orally and in writing
- Use RIM/IG program systems to identify and locate electronic records
- Document the use of record and search techniques
- Create and use "saved searches" for recurring tasks

Monitor onsite and offsite physical inventories to ensure protection from unauthorized access by identifying and correcting discrepancies. (010213)

Knowledge of:

- Organizational policies and procedures
- Filing procedures and inventory tracking systems
- RIM/IG operating practices
- Basic auditing skills
- Organizational staff and limitations on their access to record groups

Skills:

- Communicate appropriately for the task orally and in writing
- Think analytically
- Solve problems
- Work collaboratively
- Provide customer service

Register/accession records according to organizational/RIM/IG procedures to begin the RIM/IG process. (010214)

Knowledge of:

- Records registration/accession principles and techniques
- Organizational RIM/IG program requirements and procedures for records registration/accession

Skills:

- Access records, groups of records, and records systems according to established procedures

Perform functions to consolidate or close files in accordance with established RIM/IG procedures. (010215)

Knowledge of:

- Program review and analysis
- Repository (electronic) processes
- Repository and inventory (physical) processes
- Classification system (retention codes, privacy requirements, and security levels)
- Filing methods and procedures
- Creator/end user requirements
- RIM/IG policies and procedures

Skills:

- Identify issues arising from the procedural review
- Provide policy and guidelines recommendations to management
- Summarize feedback and results
- Apply legal holds based on defined requirements

Conduct components of a records inventory by gathering data, surveying the organization, and reviewing business processes as directed. (010216)

Knowledge of:

- Organization's work processes and records that could/should be created
- Basic records inventory processes
- Generally Accepted Recordkeeping Principles® and best practices
- Basic records appraisal principles
- Vital records classification
- Database programs and appropriate forms
- RIM/IG tracking and management of enterprise content management applications
- Data map (or data atlas) of organizational systems
- Protected information (e.g., personally identifiable information, sensitive personally identifiable information, personal health information) and its recordkeeping requirements

Skills:

- Work under direction and supervision
- Analyze collected information and present the findings to RIM management
- Compile and summarize data, including record categories expected but not found

Perform tasks that support the organization's litigation requirements. (010217)

Knowledge of:

- Legal hold process, including notification, preservation, and release
- Electronic and hard copy repositories likely to contain potentially relevant records and information
- Steps to identify and preserve potentially relevant records and information
- Importance of legal and regulatory requirements
- Confidentiality requirements

Skills:

- Follow organizational policies and procedures
- Identify conflicting task instructions and notify management about them
- Verify the appropriateness of authorization
- Provide customer service
- Communicate the disposition hold process with stakeholders, orally and in writing
- Document steps taken to implement legal holds, release the hold, and disposition the records after the hold is released.

Destroy, delete, or transfer information assets in accordance with RIM/IG policies and procedures to meet the organization's compliance requirements. (010218)

Knowledge of:

- Organizational policy and practices for these activities
- Destruction methods and procedures for various storage media
- Security and privacy requirements
- Policies and practices for transferring records to archival institutions, when applicable
- Destruction equipment (e.g., shredders, pulverizers)
- Disposition authorization procedures
- Disposition certification practices
- Applicable standards and requirements to maintain destruction equipment and ensure complete physical and digital destruction of information assets

Skills:

- Think analytically
- Solve problems
- Operate destruction equipment (e.g., shredders, pulverizers)
- Communicate effectively for the task, orally and in writing
- Perform disposition queries and prepare information assets for disposition approval
- Collect metrics that support privacy program requirements for the destruction of data
- Document actions taken

Protect inactive and/or archival records by monitoring environmental controls and preventing unauthorized access following established procedures. (010219)

Knowledge of:

- Media-specific preservation practices
- Environmental controls and industry standards (e.g., fire suppression, temperature, relative humidity)
- Building access and security policy

Skills:

- Monitor environmental equipment
- Observe security and privacy protocols
- Monitor access control

Assist with audits of records for internal RIM compliance. (010220)

Knowledge of:

- RIM/IG systems, policies, and procedures
- In-house audit policy and procedures
- Quality-control policy and procedures

Skills:

- Collect and assess qualitative and quantitative data
- Identify program gaps and make recommendations to management for program improvement
- Refer suspected audit violations to the internal audit team for corrective action
- Provide supporting metrics to privacy and information security programs

Retrieve vital records to support resumption of business activities. (010221)

Knowledge of:

- Business continuity program and practice (i.e., for disaster prevention, response, recovery, and resumption of business)
- Organizational business continuity plan, key players, and specific assignments
- Recovery vendors
- Vital records program and practices
- Organizational business resumption and restoration procedures

Skills:

- Communicate appropriately for the task, orally and in writing
- Follow business continuity plans and demonstrate initiative

Perform tasks that support the organization's knowledge management efforts. (010222)

Knowledge of:

- Organizational definition of knowledge management and its impacts on RIM and IG

Skills:

- Think analytically
- Contribute to the team work ethic
- Contribute to collective knowledge

Domain: Risk Management

Risk Management: This domain pertains to the knowledge and skills necessary to proactively mitigate and manage the potential for damage, loss, or unauthorized access to information assets. Two risk management components – risk analysis, which identifies the probabilities that information will be damaged or lost, and risk assessment, which examines known or anticipated risk to information – are key concepts to systematically controlling the level of risk exposure of an organization. Additional risk management components from an operational perspective are business continuity, disaster preparedness and recovery, information privacy and security requirements, and auditing.

Level 1

Support the security of information assets by following organizational policy. (010301)

Knowledge of:

- RIM security principles and practices
- Organizational and RIM security requirements, policies, and procedures
- Organizational security classification protocols
- Organizational privacy policies and procedures
- Organizational key players within each section of the organization

Skills:

- Provide customer service conducive to the security of the records
- Adhere to RIM security procedures
- Verify requestors' security credentials

Follow procedures to protect the integrity and authenticity of information. (010302)

Knowledge of:

- Security and access controls
- Data-quality practices and conventions
- Confidentiality requirements
- Privacy policies and procedures
- Identification of protected information
- Organizational metadata standards and processes

Skills:

- Enter and proof metadata
- Handle and transport confidential records

Participate in implementation of disaster recovery plans to ensure records are available after a business disruption. (010303)

Knowledge of:

- Organizational business continuity plan (i.e., for disaster prevention, response, recovery, and resumption of business) and specific assignments
- Recovery techniques and vendors
- Vital records program and practices
- Business continuity systems and tools

Skills:

- Communicate effectively with disaster recovery team and stakeholders, orally and in writing
- Follow the business continuity plan and demonstrate initiative as required

Participate in disaster recovery drills as directed in accordance with the organization's disaster recovery plan. (010304)

Knowledge of:

- Organizational disaster recovery plan and specific assignments
- Recovery techniques

Skills:

- Respond to problems in a crisis
- Work under extreme time constraints and conditions
- Provide feedback on improvements
- Communicate appropriately for the task, orally and in writing
- Follow the plan and demonstrate initiative as required
- Prioritize tasks

Collect metrics on compliance audits and present the results to RIM management. (010305)

Knowledge of:

- Basic auditing and/or self-assessment processes
- Defined metrics to be collected
- Tools and technology resources used to collect the metrics

Skills:

- Collect metrics
- Communicate effectively for the task, orally and in writing
- Document findings for future reference

Describe how security and privacy principles are incorporated into the RIM program. (010306)

Knowledge of:

- Organizational security and privacy policies and procedures
- Identification of protected information
- Physical and digital locations of protected information
- Data processing and controlling requirements for protected information

Skills:

- Communicate appropriately about access, restrictions, security, and privacy of information
- Understand the risks related to privacy and security
- Escalate issues or potential issues appropriately to the right audiences
- Simplify RIM concepts for end user training and explanations

Domain: Communications and Marketing

Communications and Marketing: This domain pertains to the knowledge and skills necessary to effectively exchange thoughts, messages, or information by speech, writing, or behavior and to effectively champion the benefits of a RIM program within an organization or to external stakeholders. The domain covers training and education of users about the RIM program. The Communications and Marketing domain is vital to developing successful business relationships to maximize RIM support and compliance, communicate the importance of RIM, and promote the value of RIM principles and best practices.

Level I

Communicate with customers and co-workers to provide effective customer service.
(010401)

Knowledge of:

- RIM processes and services offered and how they support the organization and its departments
- Organizational operation and structure
- Organizational and RIM-related services
- RIM team's expertise
- Business communication tools used in the organization

Skills:

- Communicate appropriately for the task, orally and in writing
- Provide customer service
- Treat customers and co-workers with dignity, respect, and fairness
- Solve problems
- Encourage change through personal communications

Domain: Information Technology

Information Technology: This domain pertains to the knowledge and skills necessary to select, assist with configuration, maintain, and use information processing systems, software applications, and supporting services or hardware and networks for the processing and distribution of data. Examples of information technology tasks in this context include the RIM software application, reprographics and imaging equipment, and electronic repositories within a specific business unit and limited in scope.

Level I

Provide input for selecting software to best support the RIM program. (010501)

Knowledge of:
- Current IT platform and applications used to access various physical and digital repositories
- Terminology used in records classification, taxonomies, and schemes
- End user challenges and difficulties in using current systems
- Basic RIM principles
- Basic search methodologies
- RIM program requirements

Skills:
- Communicate appropriately for the task, orally and in writing
- Assess end user needs for information
- Communicate the value of the system or application to the end user and to IT

Increase record repositories' efficiency by performing data normalization, cleanup, and reconciliation activities. (010502)

Knowledge of:
- Data entry specifications and procedures to ensure accuracy and integrity of the data, whether in electronic or physical form
- Applicable software to increase efficiency
- Data specifications to support digital preservation and ensure usability of the data as the quantity grows

Skills:
- Follow data entry and normalization conventions
- Interpret quality control procedures when analyzing data quality
- Analyze data quality to identify discrepancies
- Analyze information volumes as they increase

Provide reprographics, micrographics, and imaging services as directed. (010503)

Knowledge of:
- Equipment operations and maintenance
- Techniques used for image capture
- Evaluation and preparation techniques for source documents
- Quality control and auditing procedures
- Time required to process batches of information

Skills:
- Operate equipment
- Evaluate product output for quality assurance
- Report project status to customers
- Communicate with customers to identify quality discrepancies
- Follow quality control procedures when auditing data quality
- Identify possible process improvement

Use technology effectively in support of the RIM program. (010504)

Knowledge of:

- Computer-based tools
- Application program interfaces
- Typical office productivity software (e.g., Microsoft Office suite or similar open source products)
- Command syntax for routinely used applications
- Importance of accurately performing work to meet objectives

Skills:

- Use software to achieve work objectives
- Use input and output devices
- Document and record information
- Identify and locate information using available technology
- Categorize and organize information
- Identify and correct data entry errors
- Store documents in their proper physical or digital locations

Domain: Leadership

Leadership: This domain pertains to the knowledge and skills necessary to increase RIM awareness and motivate groups of people toward the achievement of the RIM program goals within the context of the organization's overall goals. Effective leaders must positively influence others by using leadership skills such as guiding, motivating, mentoring, and promoting continuing education and learning; interpersonal skills such as empathy and sensitivity; creative thinking skills such as brainstorming and thinking untraditionally; and change management skills such as trust building and networking.

Level I

Perform effectively during times of organizational change. (010601)

Knowledge of:
- Organizational change
- Organizational environment and culture
- Organizational policies and procedures
- Conflict management styles and strategies

Skills:
- Adapt behavior and work methods when faced with changes
- Communicate positively with staff about the changes
- Cooperate and collaborate when change occurs

Recognize conflicts and manage relationships. (010602)

Knowledge of:
- Effects of conflict
- Cross-cultural considerations when dealing with conflict
- Personality types

Skills:
- Listen to facilitate understanding and prevent conflict
- Identify different courses of action
- Accept mediation decisions
- Demonstrate honesty and act according to ethical principles
- Sustain cooperative working relationships

Participate in team-building techniques to achieve organizational goals. (010603)

Knowledge of:
- Goal setting
- Teamwork
- Organizational policies and procedures
- Organizational goals
- Personal strengths and weaknesses

Skills:
- Develop cooperative working relationships
- Treat customers and co-workers with dignity, respect, and fairness
- Objectively consider others' ideas and opinions
- Demonstrate commitment, team spirit, pride, and trust
- Change behavior in response to constructive criticism
- Demonstrate quality work
- Demonstrate honesty and act according to ethical principles
- Deliver on commitments

Level 2: This level RIM practitioner will have prior RIM knowledge, skills, and experience. At this level, the person understands more than the basic techniques and technologies, has managed or developed records management projects, and has knowledge of information management lifecycle concepts. In addition, the practitioner may be developing specialty skills (e.g., analysis, auditing, warehousing, and application technologies) and may have experience supervising other RIM staff. Practitioners at this level generally hold an undergraduate degree, usually in a RIM-related field.

Domain: Business Functions

Business Functions: This domain pertains to the knowledge and skills necessary to administer, implement, or maintain the non-RIM specific functions an organization performs, or needs to perform, to achieve its objectives. Examples of business functions include the supervision of RIM staff, budgeting, providing customer service, identifying and mapping work processes, providing input to management, and strategic planning.

Level 2

Identify and document problems in work processes and suggest improvements to support the organization's strategic plan. (020101)

Knowledge of:

- RIM program and structure
- How the RIM program relates to relevant tasks
- Current work processes, procedures, and their rationale
- Organizational processes, policies, and procedures
- Operating budget
- Staffing requirements and expectations for output of employees

Skills:

- Identify, collect, and record appropriate data
- Assess and identify procedures that require updating
- Identify alternatives, analyze potential benefits and risks, and provide justification for the recommended solution
- Prepare reports for management review
- State objectives and strategies to support recommendations
- Demonstrate innovation and initiative in proposing solutions
- Communicate findings effectively
- Conduct statistical analysis on RIM operational efficiencies

Conduct a business process analysis to develop a conceptual model of how records relate to the organization's business and its business processes. (020102)

Knowledge of:

- Data gathering
- Process-mapping strategies
- Relevant legal and regulatory requirements
- Organizational operational environment
- Management principles and techniques
- ISO 15489-1:2016, *Information and documentation – Records management – Part 1: Concepts and principles*
- Gap analysis techniques
- Business analysis techniques

Skills:

- Interview users and stakeholders regarding business processes
- Collect and analyze data
- Organize and document findings in a systematic process
- Map business requirements to records processes
- Apply business process analysis to make decisions about records creation, capture, control, storage, and disposition
- Define, evaluate, clarify, and communicate requirements
- Identify records to be captured into the system
- Make recommendations for the length of retention periods, based on operational, fiscal, legal, and historical needs (as described in ISO 15489-1:2016, *Information and documentation – Records management – Part 1: Concepts and principles*)

Research technologies and products to recommend changes to meet business needs. (020103)

Knowledge of:

- RIM vendors and solutions
- RIM industry and professional resources
- RIM industry requirements, standards, best practices, and trends
- Relevant business functions and processes
- Relevant legal and regulatory requirements

Skills:

- Communicate appropriately for the task, orally and in writing
- Research relevant technologies, tools, and techniques
- Collect, analyze, and assimilate data
- Summarize and report findings

Help develop appropriate functional and technical requirements by interviewing stakeholders, analyzing and prioritizing their responses, and reviewing the business processes to meet the business needs. (020104)

Knowledge of:

- Data-gathering techniques
- Relevant legal and regulatory requirements
- Relevant business functions and processes
- Business operating environment
- Relevant IT practices

Skills:

- Document processes used to develop requirements
- Communicate with end users, managers, and stakeholders regarding business processes and information requirements
- Conduct testing to determine the expected vs. actual performance
- Collect, analyze, and assimilate data
- Apply RIM knowledge to practical issues
- Map findings into RIM practices and business processes

Identify recordkeeping requirements to document the business functions. (020105)

Knowledge of:
- Mandatory characteristics of reliable and authentic records
- Theory and practice of design and management of RIM systems
- Organizational business functions and RIM practices
- Requirements to ensure comprehensive, adequate, reliable, authentic records

Skills:
- Construct appropriate research methodology and processes
- Review and analyze data
- Develop recordkeeping requirements to document the functions
- Review and research the functions and RIM practices
- Communicate effectively with key stakeholders, orally and in writing

Lead and direct RIM staff work activities. (020106)

Knowledge of:
- Assigned duties of direct reports
- Outcomes and expectations of assigned projects
- Performance review process

Skills:
- Establish metrics and audit to evaluate progress
- Communicate appropriately for the task, orally and in writing

Produce status reports by assessing, reviewing, and analyzing project outcomes. (020107)

Knowledge of:
- Project management tools and techniques
- Principles of statistical analysis
- Industry trends and requirements for the organization's line of business
- Basic auditing practices

Skills:
- Conduct benchmarking against RIM best practices
- Analyze qualitative and quantitative data
- Use charts and graphs
- Collect project or program data
- Make recommendations for projects or programs to management
- Identify possible issues during the project
- Communicate effectively with stakeholders, orally and in writing
- Conduct project risk analysis

Provide input for organizational policies and guidelines by analyzing the processes. (020108)

Knowledge of:
- Workflow
- Software applications used in business processes
- RIM best practices
- RIM program requirements
- Current policies and practices

Skills:
- Research and collect project or program data
- Make policy and guideline recommendations to management
- Assess process effectiveness with respect to the program goals and requirements
- Create clear documentation of the policy and process

Monitor and report changes in the organizational business environment that have an impact on the creation and use of records. (020109)

Knowledge of:
- RIM principles and best practices
- Organizational and RIM program policies and procedures
- Business functions and changes
- Survey and evaluation techniques
- Auditing techniques

Skills:
- Monitor RIM systems and organizational changes with a view to identifying significant impacts in a RIM context
- Communicate effectively with key stakeholders, orally and in writing

Provide customer service for the organization, including for requests for information, analysis, and RIM services to meet the business objectives. (020110)

Knowledge of:
- Customer service goals and delivery
- Organizational business products and services
- Communication tools and techniques
- Staffing hierarchy and corporate culture
- Conflict resolution tools and techniques
- Interpersonal dynamics
- Privacy and security standards for RIM
- Records access requirements

Skills:
- Communicate appropriately for the task, orally and in writing
- Manage time
- Resolve conflicts
- Collaborate with colleagues and customers to meet business needs
- Maximize use of technology for information access

Respond to complex requests that require research. (020111)

Knowledge of:
- Tools and techniques used for records retrieval and other end user services
- RIM program policies and procedures
- Records research principles and strategies
- Organizational requirements for security, classification, and access
- Advanced search techniques and processes
- Reference interview techniques
- Data processing and controlling requirements for protected information
- Privacy requirements that affect release of information

Skills:
- Identify and locate records
- Use RIM program systems to identify and produce records in response to user requests
- Use RIM program systems and records to provide users with information
- Solve problems
- Perform detailed research into records
- Search, find, and deliver records
- Track and monitor records in circulation
- Identify closed records and prevent their unauthorized access
- Document record use

Classify and process incoming information according to RIM procedures to meet organizational compliance requirements. (020112)

Knowledge of:

- Distribution requirements
- Security and privacy requirements for processing incoming information
- Customer service practices
- Appropriate distribution technologies
- Applicable time requirements affecting information processing or compliance

Skills:

- Document processes used to meet compliance requirements
- Create distribution schedules
- Coordinate special delivery practices to clients

Domain: RIM/IG Practices

RIM/IG Practices: This domain pertains to the knowledge and skills required to systematically manage information assets from creation or receipt through processing, distributing, sharing, using, accessing, organizing, storing and retrieving, and disposing of them. Information is a vital organizational asset, and organizations depend on accurate, complete, and readily available information to assist in making decisions; providing litigation support; improving organizational efficiency; documenting compliance with legislative, regulatory, contractual, and audit requirements; and providing historical reference.

Level 2

Assess and recommend appropriate media and practices for the RIM/IG program.
(020201)

Knowledge of:

- Legal and policy frameworks governing the organization and IG
- RIM program requirements
- Current and evolving technologies and their applications
- End-user expectations and business needs
- Concepts, techniques, technologies, and roles associated with IG

Skills:

- Identify and communicate to stakeholders and end users the benefits associated with adopting IG principles and solutions
- Analyze methods to meet evolving end-user expectations and business needs
- Communicate appropriately for the task, orally and in writing
- Present findings to key stakeholders

Conduct research to provide input into the design of ECM systems. (020202)

Knowledge of:

- Organizational structure and infrastructure
- Business mission, objectives, and strategy
- Industry standards
- Research techniques
- Sources of information and standards on RIM/IG
- Laws, regulations, and compliance requirements
- Business and end-user requirements

Skills:

- Identify relevant sources of information
- Determine functional needs of the stakeholders
- Apply theories and concepts to support a compliant enterprise content management systems design
- Organize, analyze, and interpret information
- Design research strategies
- Provide feedback to IT, orally and in writing

Help design RIM/IG programs by correlating business processes and legal and operational issues to the RIM/IG requirements. (020203)

Knowledge of:

- Organizational legal and regulatory environment
- Laws, regulations, and compliance requirements
- RIM / IG programs and policies
- Organizational operational environment
- Management principles and techniques
- Organizational e-discovery procedures
- Business group functions
- Data processing and controlling requirements

Skills:

- Revise policies and procedures as directed
- Analyze the impact of recommended changes on staff and staffing requirements and on compliance
- Document the electronic and physical workflows
- Communicate effectively with peers and stakeholders, orally and in writing

Survey the RIM/IG program by business unit function and requirements to ensure compliance. (020204)

Knowledge of:

- Business functions and organizational information assets
- RIM/IG standards, best practices, and industry trends
- Business processes
- RIM/IG program and related applications
- Organizational legal and regulatory requirements
- Generally Accepted Recordkeeping Principles® and best practices
- Auditing practices

Skills:

- Analyze data and translate it into useable information
- Benchmark practices with similar organizations
- Identify program gaps and recommend program improvement
- Recommend changes to comply with legal/regulatory, contractual, and audit requirements; business needs; and RIM/IG best practices
- Document process used and lessons learned

Make recommendations on drafting RIM/IG policies and procedures by reviewing and analyzing RIM/IG systems and requirements in line with RIM/IG best practices. (020205)

Knowledge of:

- Current RIM/IG theory, standards, and best practices
- Organizational RIM/IG practices and requirements
- Organizational legal and regulatory environment and compliance requirements
- IG best practices

Skills:

- Communicate appropriately for the task, orally and in writing
- Communicate RIM/IG requirements to stakeholders, orally and in writing
- Document recommendations and supporting rationale for future reference

Develop procedures for describing information assets and the systems and environments that create or receive them. (020206)

Knowledge of:

- RIM/IG theory, standards, and best practices
- Archival description theory and best practices
- Archives collections policy
- Context of records to organizational functions and history
- Methodology development and procedure writing

Skills:

- Communicate appropriately for the task, orally and in writing
- Document the context of the physical archival environment
- Research and apply to the business best RIM practices and procedures, as feasible
- Document the context of the RIM/IG systems
- Draft procedures

Lead and direct help desk responses for RIM/IG applications and programs. (020207)

Knowledge of:

- Customer relationship management
- Technologies specific to the RIM/IG applications that are supported
- RIM/IG program and practices

Skills:

- Communicate appropriately for the task, orally and in writing
- Collect and analyze end user service requests
- Think critically
- Provide customer service
- Ability to explain RIM concepts and terminology to non-specialists

Develop and maintain professional, industry, and organizational knowledge to serve as a subject matter expert. (020208)

Knowledge of:

- Applicable industry and professional organizations
- Industry and professional resources
- Industry trends and best practices
- RIM industry trends and requirements
- Business functions and processes
- Legal and regulatory requirements
- Knowledge management program and functions

Skills:

- Communicate appropriately for the task, orally and in writing
- Research applicable technologies, tools, and techniques
- Collaborate with teams and communities of practice
- Collect, synthesize, and assimilate data
- Apply theory and knowledge to practices
- Think critically and clearly
- Identify changes in business operations, regulatory requirements, and technology

Develop specific task instructions to enable end users to follow established RIM/IG procedures. (020209)

Knowledge of:

- Daily tasks and proper sequence
- Generally Accepted Recordkeeping Principles® and best practices
- RIM/IG organizational practices

Skills:

- Communicate appropriately for the task, orally and in writing
- Communicate the task sequence of RIM/IG processes effectively
- Understand user needs while applying RIM/IG principles and best practices
- Implement RIM/IG processes effectively

Provide RIM/IG program and policy training. (020210)

Knowledge of:

- Training methodologies and techniques
- Group and interpersonal dynamics
- Research techniques and strategies
- Learning styles and strategies
- Compliance requirements
- Audit requirements

Skills:

- Develop and deliver training presentations to end users
- Give and accept constructive feedback
- Use self-directed learning techniques
- Assess training quality and feedback
- Implement ongoing improvement strategies for training development
- Provide customer service
- Coordinate with the compliance officer to ensure legal requirements are met
- Coordinate with the internal audit team to ensure audit requirements are met

Provide input for template revisions, oversight, and guidance to end users. (020211)

Knowledge of:

- Fundamentals of template design, structure, function, and usage
- IT principles and applications
- Business documentation processes
- Organizational regulatory, legal, and contractual environment and requirements
- User interface design
- Graphic design

Skills:

- Analyze template usage
- Communicate appropriately for the task, orally and in writing
- Summarize information
- Help develop a template policy and guidelines
- Conduct surveys and employ feedback related to end user experience
- Use graphics design applications
- Maintain a repository of templates and a template history

Help develop RIM/IG system specifications by using best practices, assessing business needs, and clearly documenting requirements. (020212)

Knowledge of:

- Mandatory characteristics, design, and management of RIM/enterprise content managemennt (ECM) systems
- IG
- Organizational business functions and RIM/IG practices
- Compliance requirements
- End-user requirements and expectations

Skills:

- Review, research, and analyze data and metadata requirements
- Articulate the requirements for RIM/ECM systems
- Help design RIM/ECM systems
- Communicate the compliance requirements
- Design, test, redesign, and implement RIM/ECM systems

Help develop an information assets classification scheme and associated file plans. (020213)

Knowledge of:

- File classification schemes and file plans
- Organizational taxonomies, controlled language, and file-naming conventions
- Organizational RIM/IG requirements
- Organizational business strategy, tactics, and priorities
- Organizational business functions
- Business needs and RIM/IG best practices

Skills:

- Construct and document classification schemes
- Develop and document file plans
- Gather data on information assets and business functions and translate them into subject hierarchies and sets of rules

Help develop, implement, and use the information assets classification scheme. (020214)

Knowledge of:

- Organizational structure, infrastructure, and workflow
- Information governance trends
- Organizational RIM/IG requirements
- Information management/ECM system design
- Classification processes, schemes, and techniques
- Legal and policy frameworks governing the organization and its information management
- RIM/IG principles and best practices

Skills:

- Apply a classification design scheme
- Communicate effectively with stakeholders, orally and in writing
- Communicate compliance requirements
- Consult with business groups and end users on the design of classification schemes
- Apply technical knowledge to develop and maintain easily accessible systems and procedures

Research, develop, revise, and monitor a controlled vocabulary (e.g., thesauri, taxonomies). (020215)

Knowledge of:

- Thesaurus construction and taxonomy
- Organizational business functions and information assets
- RIM/IG principles and best practices
- Taxonomy software, enterprise content managemennt system taxonomy, and thesaurus capabilities

Skills:

- Develop, maintain, revise, and document thesauri and taxonomies
- Gather and translate data on information assets and business functions into subject hierarchies and sets of rules
- Review anomalies to determine the changes that are needed
- Communicate appropriately for the task, orally and in writing
- Consult with end users to analyze information assets and business requirements and processes

Direct the processing of information assets involved with mergers, acquisitions, divestitures, and reorganizations by applying classification and taxonomy schemes so information assets are handled using established controls and processes. (020216)

Knowledge of:

- Organizational structures
- Inventory processes for information assets, both electronic and physical
- Vital records classifications of all involved organizations
- Legal and regulatory requirements of all involved organizations
- Database programs and appropriate forms
- Software applications in use
- Terminology used in classification, taxonomies, and schemes for information assets
- Physical records transportation and logistics
- Data mapping
- Security of records containing protected information

Skills:

- Analytical thinking
- Organize and analyze collected data
- Document classification and taxonomy schemes
- Solve problems
- Communicate appropriately for the task, orally and in writing
- Communicate compliance requirements
- Relate with stakeholders and end users
- Recognize and resolve conflicting data prior to data entry or merging
- Organize record center relocation and office moves
- Manage stakeholder requirements for protected information

Help develop policies and procedures for version control within and across media. (020217)

Knowledge of:

- Issues surrounding the management of versions in business environments
- Contractual requirements
- Strategies, policies, and procedures to control version creation and maintenance
- Organizational RIM/IG practices for copying and maintaining duplicate records
- RIM/IG theory and best practices
- Workflow and collaboration methodologies
- Compliance requirements and protection of information from unauthorized access

Skills:

- Analyze data
- Communicate appropriately for the task, orally and in writing
- Train end users on policy adherence and practical application

Appraise information assets for inclusion in a RIM/IG/archives program. (020218)

Knowledge of:

- Appraisal principles and techniques
- Organizational RIM/IG program requirements, procedures, and retention schedules
- Organizational archives collections policy
- Organizational classification scheme

Skills:

- Accession records according to RIM/IG/archival program procedures
- Facilitate the electronic and/or physical transfer of records to archives
- Assess information assets to assign their classification metadata
- Document process followed during the appraisal

Appraise and analyze recorded information for retention purposes, as directed. (020219)

Knowledge of:

- Classification schemes and record series used in retention scheduling
- RIM/IG program and all its components
- Organizational appraisal and collection policies and practices
- Current repositories and archival holdings
- Structure of records retention schedule
- Criteria used to identify records with archival value

Skills:

- Think analytically
- Organize and analyze collected data
- Document analysis findings and resulting decisions
- Communicate findings to stakeholders effectively, orally and in writing

Identify duplicate records across media by reviewing workflow, current practices, and record content. (020220)

Knowledge of:

- Theory and practice of duplicate creation and management
- RIM/IG program requirements, policies, and procedures for duplicate management
- Deduplication software functionality

Skills:

- Apply software applications to identify potential duplicates
- Monitor and analyze findings to identify problems and non-compliance issues
- Comply with duplicate management procedures
- Report records duplication issues and suggest solutions
- Communicate findings to stakeholders

Identify retention series and create descriptions after analyzing the information assets to be incorporated into the RIM/IG and archives programs. (020221)

Knowledge of:

- Advanced principles of records and archives documentation, collection, and description techniques
- Organizational business functions
- RIM/IG and archives programs' requirements with respect to the description of information assets
- Context of information assets to organizational functions

Skills:

- Create metadata profiles for electronic and physical information assets
- Conduct electronic and physical inventories of organizational information assets

Develop retention schedules by evaluating records and non-records series according to business function. (020222)

Knowledge of:
- Business functions and organizational information assets
- Organizational legal and regulatory environments and requirements
- Archival collections policy and appraisal practices
- RIM/IG principles and best practices
- Privacy and security standards for records
- Evidential, informational, and historical value of records
- Organizational contractual and audit obligations

Skills:
- Collect and analyze data
- Evaluate records and non-records against business, legal, regulatory, and archival requirements
- Communicate appropriately for the task, orally and in writing
- Develop clear and concise retention schedules
- Distinguish systems of record from locations with incomplete or obsolete document versions
- Research federal, state, and local laws and regulations that address recordkeeping requirements

Gather information from stakeholders and end users during periodic updates of retention schedules. (020223)

Knowledge of:
- RIM/IG principles and best practices
- Business needs for retention beyond legal and regulatory requirements
- Various models for structuring retention schedules and the pros and cons of each mode (e.g., granular series, "big bucket," departmental, functional schedules)
- Potential historic, intrinsic, or enduring value of information
- Legal research techniques

Skills:
- Calculate trigger events for records series
- Identify ends of retention periods and disposition
- Communicate effectively with stakeholders, orally and in writing
- Identify changes in business operations and compliance and audit requirements specific to the organization
- Document rationale for changes made to the schedule

Review retention schedules prior to implementing disposition actions. (020224)

Knowledge of:
- Information assets appraisal
- Business processes and requirements
- Privacy and security standards for information assets
- Statutes, regulations, and contractual considerations
- Media composition and destruction/recycling industry standards and processes
- Evidential, informational, and historical values of information assets

Skills:
- Create concise and comprehensive documentation on the disposition review and approval process
- Communicate effectively with stakeholders, orally and in writing
- Research, interpret, and apply laws, regulations, and contractual obligations
- Identify, certify, and track information assets for destruction and other disposition actions
- Follow the destruction authorization process
- Implement, maintain, and release legal holds and other preservation orders
- Match records and non-records to the series that are detailed in retention schedules
- Identify, document, and resolve anomalies and exceptions

Identify records having potential archival value. (020225)

Knowledge of:

- Principles and practices of archives management
- RIM/IG program and practice with respect to the management of archives
- Organizational archives collections policy

Skills:

- Understand the rationale for the preservation of archival records and artifacts (including pictures and videos)
- Understand rationales for access, and access restrictions, to archival records

Review and update records retention schedules on a routine basis. (020226)

Knowledge of:

- Record appraisal
- Business processes and requirements
- Organization's regulatory and legal requirements and environment
- Organization's structure and functions
- Privacy and security standards for information assets
- Research and information collection methodology
- Organizational contractual obligations
- Archival theory and practices

Skills:

- Identify and document new retention schedule series and their disposition
- Identify obsolete retention schedule series for decommissioning
- Review and update existing records and non-records series and retention requirements
- Analyze and identify record and non-record characteristics
- Create concise and comprehensive documentation on the review schedule and process
- Research and interpret industry standards, case law, regulations, statutes, and contractual obligations
- Appraise and establish records and non-records retention periods and dispositions
- Conduct an inventory of information assets in all storage media

Identify records containing PII, SPII, or PHI. (020227)

Knowledge of:

- Jurisdictional privacy laws and requirements
- Use of personally identifiable information (PII), sensitive personally identifiable information (SPII), and protected health information (PHI) in organizational information assets
- Online data storage solutions
- Organizational policies related to the protection of information
- Organizational location and the use of PII
- De-identification and redaction procedures
- Risk assessment

Skills:

- Manage stakeholder requirements for PII, SPII, and PHI
- Evaluate storage technology and system access controls
- Integrate special access restrictions within repositories
- Document steps taken to comply with the requirements

Comply with information security classification policy and procedures. (020228)

Knowledge of:

- Organization's legal and regulatory environment and jurisdictional requirements
- Organizational security and privacy policies and procedures
- Location(s) in which confidential information is stored

Skills:

- Evaluate information assets in accordance with security and privacy classification procedures
- Communicate records security and security classification incidents to management
- Communicate policies and procedures of the security classification regime to RIM/IG stakeholders
- Identify records that contain protected information
- Document findings for future reference

Provide guidance in centralized and decentralized file management operations to improve access and control. (020229)

Knowledge of:

- File management systems
- File management operations
- Facility capacity for weight loads and high-density storage
- File weights and floor load-bearing engineering studies
- Needs projections for future expansion
- Filing systems and equipment
- Staffing needs
- Safety requirements for operations
- RIM/IG information asset tracking and management software
- Requirements for the protection and preservation of various storage media

Skills:

- Comply with human resources requirements
- Comply with inventory control and records retrieval
- Use RIM/enterprise content management applications to manage information assets
- Apply metrics to forecast and decide on space requirements
- Manage active and inactive records
- Use retention schedules
- Recommend equipment for storage and management of records

Domain: Risk Management

Risk Management: This domain pertains to the knowledge and skills necessary to proactively mitigate and manage the potential for damage, loss, or unauthorized access to information assets. Two risk management components – risk analysis, which identifies the probabilities that information will be damaged or lost, and risk assessment, which examines known or anticipated risk to information – are key concepts to systematically controlling the level of risk exposure of an organization. Additional risk management components from an operational perspective are business continuity, disaster preparedness and recovery, information privacy and security requirements, and auditing.

Level 2

Help perform a risk assessment by identifying and prioritizing risks relating to records. (020301)

Knowledge of:

- Organizational business continuity plans (i.e., for disaster prevention, response, recovery, and resumption of business)
- Disaster recovery techniques
- Risk management principles
- Organizational risk assessment principles
- Organizational auditing practices and principles
- Legal research methodologies
- Basic statistical analysis principles
- Advanced spreadsheet functions
- Controls to preserve the security and protection of all information assets

Skills:

- Evaluate legal guidelines
- Collect, analyze, and assimilate relevant data
- Communicate findings and recommendations with managers and stakeholders
- Identify and evaluate risk
- Identify and develop risk mitigation techniques and strategies
- Identify program gaps and make recommendations for program improvement
- Document steps taken during the risk assessment process

Provide input to disaster planning efforts by assessing and documenting critical business processes and identifying vital records. (020302)

Knowledge of:

- Organizational business continuity plan (i.e., for disaster prevention, response, recovery, and resumption of business)
- Disaster recovery techniques and vendors
- Inventory and repository contents
- Vital records management principles
- Organizational business continuity systems and tools
- Security and protection of vital records

Skills:

- Collaborate with IT to plan and execute business continuity plans
- Schedule and prioritize recovery steps and processes
- Enter business continuity plan data in business continuity systems and tools
- Negotiate and resolve conflicts
- Communicate appropriately for the task, orally and in writing
- Assess the applicability of solutions to specific needs
- Identify and inventory vital records
- Identify the requirements for vital records management, protection, handling, storage, and reconstitution

Participate in emergency plan preparation and drills. (020303)

Knowledge of:

- Emergency planning strategies and techniques
- Disaster recovery processes
- Training methodologies and techniques
- Vital records management program
- Business continuity principles (i.e., for disaster prevention, response, recovery, and resumption of business)
- Gap analysis methodology
- Facilities and logistics
- Local and regional emergency action plans
- Team-building and motivational processes

Skills:

- Participate in disaster recovery training and drills
- Perform assigned roles and conduct role playing
- Report on the drill results
- Coordinate disaster teams and explain team responsibilities for RIM
- Identify program gaps and make recommendations to management for program improvement

Assist with security classification policies and procedures. (020304)

Knowledge of:

- Security classification theory and principles
- Security classification requirements for the organization's records
- Security classification administration principles and practices
- Privacy issues that affect the organization
- Organization's privacy policy

Skills:

- Communicate appropriately for the task, orally and in writing
- Apply the appropriate security classification to information
- Educate RIM stakeholders on the policies and procedures and monitor their compliance
- Maintain privacy checklists
- Collect information for privacy impact assessments
- Identify and update policy and procedures impacted by security classification

Help implement the records security classification policy and procedures. (020305)

Knowledge of:

- Security classification
- RIM program policy, practices, and procedures
- Security classification requirements for the organization's records
- Privacy issues that affect the organization
- Privacy requirements for records that contain protected information

Skills:

- Communicate appropriately for the task, orally and in writing
- Apply the appropriate security classification to information
- Educate RIM stakeholders on the policies and procedures and monitor their compliance
- Maintain privacy checklists
- Collect information for privacy impact assessments
- Monitor, evaluate, and promote the use of security classification schemes
- Report on incidents, triggers, and the maintenance of the security classification framework
- Incorporate privacy data handling and controlling requirements into the security classification procedures

Protect the integrity and authenticity of records. (020306)

Knowledge of:

- Security, protection, and access controls
- Data quality practices and procedures
- Access control policies and principles
- Information security requirements
- Business continuity plan (i.e., for disaster prevention, response, recovery, and resumption of business)
- Confidentiality requirements

Skills:

- Audit and review access to records
- Maintain confidential and sensitive information
- Help maintain the appropriate environmental and safety controls
- Review access list and determine if changes are needed
- Train users on steps needed to ensure records integrity and authenticity in their business processes

Assist legal counsel and management with the legal hold process. (020307)

Knowledge of:

- Organizational policies and procedures related to legal holds
- Legal and policy frameworks governing information management
- Electronic devices that may contain data
- Previous and current RIM compliance issues
- Security and protection controls for records in a legal hold
- *The Sedona Conference® 2010 Commentary on Legal Holds: The Trigger & The Process*
- Forms and documentation related to disposition
- Legacy and orphaned systems that may contain information assets
- Data storage practices and media
- Organizational security and privacy policies and procedures
- Document production and document discovery/e-discovery requirements
- Training methodologies and techniques

Skills:

- Provide internal and external customer service
- Create status reports
- Identify the scope of the records affected
- Process the affected records
- Assist with the resumption process for removing the legal hold
- Create disposition reports
- Train the staff on legal hold processes and procedures
- Apply legal holds
- Communicate effectively the needs and compliance requirements of the legal hold, orally and in writing
- Process the legal hold checks for offboarding staff

Safeguard vital records identified within the vital records program. (020308)

Knowledge of:

- Vital records management program
- Backup tools and techniques
- Related IT principles and applications
- Safeguarding recordkeeping systems
- Business objectives and requirements
- Business continuity principles (i.e., for disaster prevention, response, recovery, and resumption of business)
- Disaster preparedness and recovery methodologies

Skills:

- Interpret business processes and functions
- Identify gaps and redundancies in vital records storage
- Collaborate with IT to identify systems containing vital records that may require special protection
- Train end users on how vital records are protected

Domain: Communications and Marketing

Communications and Marketing: This domain pertains to the knowledge and skills necessary to effectively exchange thoughts, messages, or information by speech, writing, or behavior and to effectively champion the benefits of a RIM program within an organization or to external stakeholders. The domain covers training and education of users about the RIM program. The Communications and Marketing domain is vital to developing successful business relationships to maximize RIM support and compliance, communicate the importance of RIM, and promote the value of RIM principles and best practices.

Level 2

Communicate with stakeholders to determine RIM needs. (020401)

Knowledge of:

- Organizational structure, business strategy, policies, and objectives
- Information management system design
- Legal and policy frameworks governing the organization and its information management
- Survey and focus group techniques
- RIM program goals, systems, and procedures
- Records center policies and practices

Skills:

- Communicate appropriately for the task, orally and in writing
- Develop and deliver presentations using various media for target audiences
- Organize, analyze, and interpret information
- Present and defend viable recommendations from data collections, research, and analysis
- Motivate others during organizational change processes
- Document RIM needs and stakeholder input

Collaborate with stakeholders to achieve compliance with the RIM program. (020402)

Knowledge of:

- Business partners and stakeholders' goals and objectives
- Organizational mission, vision, goals, and objectives
- RIM program system, goals, strategy, and benefits
- Strategic planning
- Concerns of oversight bodies
- Internal resources
- Public relations
- Industry issues for which IG facilitates organizational governance
- Value of RIM to other organizational activities

Skills:

- Explain the value of the RIM program to the organization
- Control the quality of RIM processes
- Assess, analyze, and correct data in line with RIM program best practices and requirements
- Accept mediation decisions
- Demonstrate honesty and act according to ethical principles
- Develop and deliver presentations using various media for the target audiences
- Organize, analyze, and interpret information
- Communicate appropriately for the task, orally and in writing

Develop, maintain, and improve relationships with information technologists, internal customers, and other stakeholders. (020403)

Knowledge of:

- Communication tools and techniques
- Industry trends and RIM profession requirements
- Staffing hierarchy and corporate culture
- Conflict resolution tools and techniques
- Customer relationship management
- Interpersonal dynamics
- Related IT principles and applications
- Business objectives and requirements

Skills:

- Communicate effectively with stakeholders, verbally and in writing
- Analyze personalities and team dynamics
- Analyze the organization chart to understand management accountability and decision-making
- Model and analyze the business processes

Domain: Information Technology

Information Technology: This domain pertains to the knowledge and skills at the intermediate level necessary to develop, maintain, and use information processing systems, software applications, and supporting hardware and networks for the processing and distribution of data. Examples of information technology tasks in this context include the RIM software application, developing IT requirements for managing electronic repositories, information security, digitization, identifying technology options, and understanding stakeholder functions within the scope of one or more business unit and / or business processes.

Level 2

Help design information management systems by translating records processes into functional requirements. (020501)

Knowledge of:

- Available information management systems and technology
- Advanced best practices in RIM processes
- Principles for information-gathering requirements
- Business process analysis techniques
- Organizational legal and regulatory environment, including the drivers that require the organization to control and audit its information assets, and any multi-jurisdictional privacy requirements
- Scoring techniques to evaluate technology vendors
- Gap analysis methodology
- Policy and procedure writing for knowledge transfer initiatives
- RIM industry standards (e.g., DoD 5015.2, VERS, MoReq2010)
- Cross-functional team strategies and behaviors
- Automation solutions and functions for declaration and classification

Skills:

- Analyze records and business processes
- Determine the metadata necessary for records retrieval and authentication
- Conceptualize and visualize complex processes into practical solutions
- Perform workflow analyses
- Perform gap analyses
- Organize information into a systematic process
- Map the business and records processes
- Define, evaluate, and clarify functional and technical requirements for a gap analysis
- Create a communication plan for initiatives and projects
- Create a change management plan for RIM awareness that is aligned with the communications plan
- Incorporate privacy requirements into the system configuration

Collaborate with IT to incorporate recordkeeping requirements into systems design or upgrade. (020502)

Knowledge of:

- Business processes and functions, including use cases for common business process scenarios
- Management principles and techniques to initiate and complete projects
- Broad range of RIM practices and procedures that will achieve business goals and objectives, including archival preservation
- Organizational goals and strategic direction
- ISO 15489-1:2016, *Information and documentation – Records management – Part 1: Concepts and principles*
- RIM awareness and change management best practices
- Retention and privacy requirements unique to protected information
- Software design methodologies (e.g., agile, waterfall)

Skills:

- Communicate effectively with stakeholders, orally and in writing
- Present and market recommendations to peers and stakeholders
- Apply theory and knowledge to RIM practices
- Organize information into stages of a business process workflow
- Negotiate and resolve conflicts and priorities within and between lines of business
- Determine appropriate software design methods in response to rapidly changing technology
- Communicate the RIM business requirements to IT
- Facilitate business process re-engineering workshops

Monitor the processes for transferring or migrating records and information. (020503)

Knowledge of:

- Quality control techniques
- Records integrity and authenticity characteristics
- Record validation techniques
- Methodologies for updating, copying, and migrating information
- Privacy data processing and controlling requirements
- Legacy and current electronic document management and electronic document and records management systems
- RIM migration technologies and requirements
- Metadata standards
- Taxonomy structures and techniques
- Relevant operating systems and software

Skills:

- Utilize appropriate media
- Design and build testing criteria
- Analyze test results
- Analyze and identify record characteristics
- Recognize and reconstruct taxonomies
- Create concise and comprehensive documentation on validation and testing methods
- Perform RIM awareness and change impact analysis related to migrating records and information
- Identify quality control gaps in the extract, transform, and load (ETL) process
- Develop an ETL process for migration, based on business processes and requirements
- Perform quality reviews
- Communicate with stakeholders regarding the transfer or migration of records and any findings that require corrective action

Support and train others in the use of technology to accomplish tasks that support RIM program objectives. (020504)

Knowledge of:

- Information management systems and technologies that support RIM programs
- Technology to exchange and communicate business goals
- Methods for interacting while using technology
- Advanced search techniques and processes
- RIM training and needs assessment
- Safeguarding recordkeeping systems

Skills:

- Diagnose and solve common technology problems
- Identify areas in need of additional training
- Provide training
- Interface with regularly used applications and tools
- Interpret and analyze business problems using available technology
- Develop graphic presentations using various media
- Communicate effectively
- Evaluate input and output of others to determine accuracy
- Perform needs assessment analysis based on RIM awareness
- Develop and document a training plan

Provide input for selecting software to best support the RIM program. (020505)

Knowledge of:

- IT platform and applications, including solution functionality for access to cloud repositories and support for RIM in the cloud
- Terminology used in records classification, taxonomies, and schemes
- End user needs and expectations for search applications for multiple repositories and platforms and for the integration of applications such as enterprise resource planning and archival
- Basic RIM principles
- RIM program requirements

Skills:

- Communicate appropriately for the task, orally and in writing
- Compare and analyze software products
- Analyze end user needs for information
- Communicate the value of the system or application to the end user and to IT
- Gather and provide software, record and information classification, categorization, and disposition requirements specific to the RIM program and its end users

Domain: Leadership

Leadership: This domain pertains to the knowledge and skills necessary to increase RIM awareness and motivate groups of people toward the achievement of the RIM program goals within the context of the organization's overall goals. Effective leaders must positively influence others by using leadership skills such as guiding, motivating, mentoring, and promoting continuing education and learning; interpersonal skills such as empathy and sensitivity; creative thinking skills such as brainstorming and thinking untraditionally; and change management skills such as trust building and networking.

Level 2

Remain effective during changes in responsibilities, work environment, or other conditions affecting the organization. (020601)

Knowledge of:

- Organizational change
- Organizational environment and culture
- Organizational policies and procedures
- Conflict management styles and strategies

Skills:

- Adapt behavior and work methods when faced with changes
- Communicate positively with staff about the change
- Cooperate and collaborate during the change
- Document changes and rationale for them

Recognize conflicts and manage relationships. (020602)

Knowledge of:

- Effects of conflict
- Cross-cultural considerations when dealing with conflict
- Conflict management styles and strategies
- Personality types
- Mediation
- Ethical principles

Skills:

- Listen to facilitate understanding and prevent conflict
- Identify and recommend courses of action if the conflict should be escalated to management
- Sustain cooperative working relationships

Participate in team building to achieve organizational goals. (020603)

Knowledge of:

- Goal setting
- Teamwork
- Organizational policies and procedures
- Organizational goals
- Personal strengths and weaknesses

Skills:

- Develop cooperative working relationships
- Treat customers and co-workers with dignity, respect, and fairness
- Objectively consider others' ideas and opinions
- Demonstrate commitment, team spirit, pride, and trust
- Change individual behavior in response to constructive criticism
- Demonstrate quality work
- Demonstrate honesty and act according to ethical principles
- Take responsibility for delivering on commitments

Level 3: This level RIM practitioner is a seasoned practitioner who has worked at the enterprise level of an organization and will possess extensive knowledge of the design, creation, implementation, and management of a records management program and staff. This level of practitioner looks to high-level experts for best practices, advanced techniques, or technology innovations to learn and grow in the field. Practitioners at this level generally hold advanced degrees and/or appropriate certifications.

Domain: Business Functions

Business Functions: This domain pertains to the knowledge and skills necessary to administer, implement, or maintain the non-RIM specific functions an organization performs, or needs to perform, to achieve its objectives. Examples of business functions include the supervision of RIM staff, budgeting, providing customer service, identifying and mapping work processes, providing input to management, and strategic planning.

Level 3

Survey the business environment to optimize current and future RIM operations. (030101)

Knowledge of:

- Organizational legal and regulatory environments
- Business climate (economy, industry, and competition)
- Internal and external business processes
- Relevant sources for research
- Research techniques
- Industry best practices
- RIM industry trends
- Organizational mission, vision, and goals
- Organizational RIM program
- Budgeting and forecasting methodologies
- Relevant ISO standards
- Security and protection of recordkeeping systems

Skills:

- Comply with legal regulations that affect RIM
- Evaluate the impact of legal regulations on RIM
- Review and analyze current events for their applicability to RIM practices
- Review and analyze business processes to identify RIM needs
- Identify the organization's strengths and weaknesses relevant to international RIM standards
- Research and compile reports of recommendations for improvements
- Manage RIM components of projects

Identify and establish goals and objectives of the RIM program to support the organization's strategic plan. (030102)

Knowledge of:

- Business plan development process
- Organizational strategic plan
- Available resources (e.g., finances, personnel, equipment)

Skills:

- Analyze organizational goals for providing supporting RIM functions
- Perform a formal needs, or gap, analysis
- Prioritize relevant goals to achieve the overall mission
- Plan the activities necessary to achieve objectives
- Manage the process to support objectives
- Document RIM goals and objectives and how they support the organization's strategic plan
- Assess organizational capabilities to achieve the strategic plan

Validate and ensure that work outputs align with business plans and strategic objectives. (030103)

Knowledge of:

- RIM best practices
- Program and project planning, analysis, and reporting
- Communication techniques
- Organizational strategic plan and related business plans
- Organizational structure
- Project scope
- Project planning documentation

Skills:

- Identify gaps and issues in work products
- Document gaps and issues for future reference
- Provide constructive feedback
- Approve the final work products

Provide strategic information to management to show accountability and build coalitions across the organization. (030104)

Knowledge of:

- RIM industry trends and current events
- Competitive intelligence
- Consensus-building techniques
- Organizational structure and key players
- Gap analysis methodology

Skills:

- Analyze trends
- Present required information appropriate to each audience
- Build effective and lasting relationships
- Communicate appropriately for the task, orally and in writing, to leverage relationships

Identify opportunities for RIM process improvements. (030105)

Knowledge of:

- Business process improvement concepts and techniques
- Security and protection measures
- Legal and regulatory environments for the organization's industry
- Information collection methods
- RIM principles and best practices
- Assessment and continuous improvement methodologies
- Auditing techniques and strategies

Skills:

- Analyze data
- Research legal and regulatory environments
- Communicate effectively for the task, orally and in writing
- Identify program gaps, make recommendations to management for program improvement, and document suggested improvements

Identify projects and coordinate the resources to ensure projects succeed and organizational goals and objectives are met. (030106)

Knowledge of:

- Project management and planning processes and software tools
- Required and available resources (e.g., finances, personnel, equipment)
- Workload and ability to effect or incorporate change
- Financial resources and budgeting

Skills:

- Delegate work and manage and instruct subordinates and contractors
- Evaluate and communicate the benefits of implementing projects
- Analyze the need for program improvements and project expectations
- Prioritize multiple projects
- Develop reports and communicate project status
- Adjust project resources in response to project changes

Develop periodic reports by auditing and analyzing data and information related to the RIM program. (030107)

Knowledge of:

- Management decision-making
- Reporting techniques
- Key performance indicators
- Benchmarking methodology
- Organizational structure and processes
- Industry standards and best practices
- RIM program strategy and goals
- Program and project planning, analysis, and reporting
- Auditing techniques and strategies

Skills:

- Present complex concepts
- Identify and apply key performance indicators
- Communicate appropriately for the task, orally and in writing

Provide, monitor, and audit metrics for RIM program productivity and performance. (030108)

Knowledge of:

- Metrics models
- Forecasting and trend analysis
- Total quality management principles and benchmarking opportunities
- Auditing principles, techniques, and methodologies
- How RIM principles support organizational operations
- Key inputs, outputs, and other measures
- Project management tools and techniques
- Customer relationship management

Skills:

- Identify synergies and economics of scale based on metric analysis
- Discern what to measure
- Provide accurate snapshots of departmental operations, status markers, and productivity levels
- Develop reports to communicate information
- Interpret data to improve process management, make decisions, and justify and validate the program to upper management

Analyze key performance indicators and prepare reports that will help management and stakeholders demonstrate the success of the RIM program. (030109)

Knowledge of:

- Key performance indicators (e.g., budget variances, corrective actions from audits, incident reporting)
- Benchmarking methodology
- Organizational structure and processes
- RIM industry standards and best practices
- RIM program strategy and goals
- Program and project planning, analysis, and reporting
- Organizational analysis
- Stakeholders' goals and motivation

Skills:

- Identify and analyze key performance indicators
- Communicate appropriately for the task, orally and in writing
- Present information to senior-level executives and stakeholders

Review short- and long-term resources and space requirements for facility planning. (030110)

Knowledge of:

- Space planning procedures
- Records storage design parameters and best practices
- Safety and fire protection standards
- Cost/benefit analysis methodologies
- Construction estimating and scheduling
- Equipment for storage and material handling

Skills:

- Evaluate in-house operational costs relative to the estimates for outsourcing
- Review safety and fire protection plans
- Estimate space allocation and growth requirements
- Manage aspects of construction and installation projects
- Document facility recommendations and requests

Manage the process for acquiring RIM goods and services via procurement contracts. (030111)

Knowledge of:

- Procurement methodology
- Contracts management and administration
- Auditing principles and techniques
- Accounting principles and techniques
- Budget development
- Project management
- Request for information / request for proposal processes
- Vendor management
- Inventory practices and methodologies
- Master service agreements
- Software licensing options
- Outsourcing opportunities
- Requirements gathering

Skills:

- Prepare the procurement specifications and bid documents to meet the RIM program needs
- Evaluate bids for RIM goods and services to meet the program needs
- Review contracts to guarantee compliance and satisfaction of contractual obligations
- Negotiate with external suppliers
- Communicate effectively with end users, vendors, internal customers, and other stakeholders, orally and in writing
- Manage security and privacy requirements for all stakeholders when acquiring technology
- Audit the program performance against its requirements
- Assess progress and benchmark against the deliverables
- Evaluate the financial resources required for application purchase
- Perform cost/benefit analyses
- Assess vendors against criteria such as reliability, service, fitness for purpose, and value for money

Manage all aspects of the RIM budget process. (030112)

Knowledge of:

- Organizational goals and objectives
- Business functions and processes
- Organizational operational environment
- Corporate and departmental budgets
- Organizational policies and procedures for budget development and execution
- Records security and protection
- Finance and accounting principles
- Accounting and financial management applications
- Cost allocation strategies
- Cost/benefit analysis
- Forecasting and trend analysis
- Auditing principles
- Organization's procurement policies
- Master service agreements
- Management of vendors
- Outsourcing opportunities

Skills:

- Develop budgets
- Execute budgets
- Audit and evaluate finances
- Develop and use spreadsheet applications
- Interpret financial statements
- Analyze budget information for accuracy and milestone progression
- Make financial decisions in accordance with organizational goals and objectives
- Collect and analyze statistical data
- Allocate funding
- Prepare reports
- Negotiate agreements with vendors
- Develop procurement specifications and bid documents
- Assess vendors against criteria such as reliability, service, fitness for purpose, and value for money
- Communicate appropriately for the task, orally and in writing

Conduct short-term and long-range forecasting by evaluating financial conditions to meet future operational requirements. (030113)

Knowledge of:

- Organizational short-term and long-range plans and objectives

Skills:

- Develop budgets to meet short-term and long-range plans and objectives
- Implement cost allocation strategies
- Manage projects over long periods of time
- Evaluate operational needs to meet organizational goals and objectives
- Educate RIM team on business forecasting

Define roles and responsibilities for RIM staff to support the strategic plan. (030114)

Knowledge of:

- RIM requirements, policies, procedures, and processes
- RIM standards and best practices
- Organizational position description and competency requirements
- Organizational and department strategic plans
- RIM program objectives and goals
- Educational requirements for relevant positions
- Organizational levels and relevance of RIM positions

Skills:

- Assign tasks to appropriate position levels
- Analyze the skills needed for each position level
- Communicate appropriately for the task, orally and in writing
- Establish a hierarchy of positions for the RIM program
- Develop and provide sufficient training for staff development
- Align position descriptions to criteria for performance evaluations
- Develop position descriptions to meet RIM objectives

Identify RIM personnel to meet current and future staff requirements against defined position descriptions. (030115)

Knowledge of:

- Position descriptions and required competencies
- Organizational hiring policies and practices
- Reliable sources for candidates
- Succession planning
- Relevant employment laws
- Organizational remuneration packages
- Job market, referral networks, and talent pools

Skills:

- Interview candidates
- Evaluate potential candidates
- Communicate organizational policies and practices to candidates
- Evaluate the best candidates and communicate those findings
- Scan the job market for the best candidates
- Obtain buy-in from relevant parties

Develop performance criteria using defined measures for evaluating employees to determine competence. (030116)

Knowledge of:

- Staff development practices
- Motivational theory
- Organizational human resources performance and processes

Skills:

- Provide professionally constructive criticism
- Provide employee development feedback
- Review against the defined measurements
- Identify gaps and areas for improvement
- Determine appropriate employee development plans to improve performance

Recognize and use the intellectual capital of team members to enhance the quality of RIM services. (030117)

Knowledge of:

- Organizational human resource policies and procedures
- Staff strengths and weaknesses
- Level-of-service expectations
- Corporate culture
- Organizational behavior

Skills:

- Analyze the knowledge and skill base of team members
- Allocate the talent pool appropriately within RIM
- Employ the concept of teams and teamwork
- Establish and lead cross-functional teams to achieve goals
- Leverage the skills of team members

Manage the effects of change on the RIM program. (030118)

Knowledge of:

- Organizational culture
- Training methodologies and techniques
- Change management principles
- Conflict resolution management practices
- Damage control techniques

Skills:

- Mentor and encourage end users
- Educate RIM team on the impact organizational change has on the RIM program
- Solve problems
- Motivate others
- Promote the necessity of change
- Resolve conflict
- Communicate appropriately for the task, orally and in writing
- Provide leadership
- Identify and mitigate risks

Implement and manage the processes associated with regulatory obligations, industry benchmarks, and organizational requirements to achieve and demonstrate RIM compliance. (030119)

Knowledge of:

- RIM regulations, requirements, and compliance guidelines
- Litigation and regulatory environments, and their privacy requirements
- Audit principles, techniques, and methodologies
- Program audit practices and techniques
- RIM program best practices
- Active or pending actions related to information assets
- Industry trends and developments
- Benchmarking techniques, trends, and methodologies

Skills:

- Develop, perform, and improve the RIM program review
- Compile and present the audit results and recommendations to management
- Apply a gap analysis to the results to improve operations
- Research legislative and regulatory requirements
- Document the discovery request and collection methodology
- Comply with the organization's legal hold process
- Communicate appropriately for the task, orally and in writing

Manage the integration or transfer of information assets as a result of internal reorganizations, mergers, acquisitions, or divestitures. (030120)

Knowledge of:

- RIM policies and best practices
- Records and information of the business being reorganized, acquired, and/or divested
- Organizational policies, procedures, and best practices
- Potential liability and risk issues
- Organizational change
- Merger and acquisition strategy and practices
- Organizational strategic intent
- Cost control
- Resource management
- Project management tools and techniques

Skills:

- Manage projects
- Communicate appropriately for the task, orally and in writing
- Collaborate with affected parties and organizations
- Document the processes used for future RIM reference

Domain: RIM/IG Practices

RIM/IG Practices: This domain pertains to the knowledge and skills required to systematically manage information assets from creation or receipt through processing, distributing, sharing, using, accessing, organizing, storing and retrieving, and disposing of them. Information is a vital organizational asset, and organizations depend on accurate, complete, and readily available information to assist in making decisions; providing litigation support; improving organizational efficiency; documenting compliance with legislative, regulatory, contractual, and audit requirements; and providing historical reference.

Level 3

Implement systems in compliance with RIM/IG requirements based on an organizational needs analysis. (030201)

Knowledge of:

- Generally Accepted Recordkeeping Principles® and best practices
- System analysis methodologies
- RIM/IG implementation processes and procedures
- Cost/benefit analysis technologies
- Workflow processes required for implementation
- Business process analysis techniques
- Statutory, regulatory, contractual, and audit requirements
- Organizational RIM/IG practices and requirements
- Organizational legal and regulatory environments
- System industry standards (e.g., DoD5015.2, MoReq2010, VERS)
- End-user requirements and expectations

Skills:

- Identify and analyze industry trends, legal requirements, and opportunities for improvement
- Evaluate the cost of implementing systems
- Plan and organize for an enterprise content management (ECM) system implementation
- Help develop and implement RIM/IG plans for improvement
- Develop and employ evaluation tools
- Apply metrics to measure the success and impact of RIM/IG processes and systems adoption
- Document workflows and encourage their adoption and incorporation with an ECM system
- Train and facilitate to encourage end user adoption
- Communicate appropriately for the task, orally and in writing
- Obtain buy-in from the stakeholders and end users
- Conduct surveys to incorporate end-user requirements into the user interface

Develop comprehensive procedures to document organizational RIM/IG practices. (030202)

Knowledge of:

- RIM/IG policies and related processes
- Generally Accepted Recordkeeping Principles® and best practices
- Impact of change on current business processes
- Evaluation methodologies
- Business process analysis and re-engineering practices
- Knowledge management
- Procedure writing and flowcharting
- Organizational writing styles
- Records coordinator role and network

Skills:

- Communicate appropriately for the task, orally and in writing
- Collaborate with records coordinators, communities of practice, and other end users
- Oversee the development and implementation of written instructions
- Identify and reconcile individual and role-based training needs
- Document the operational processes
- Write procedures based on organizational policies and accepted style
- Educate RIM team and end users on changes in RIM/IG practices

Create and implement RIM/IG policies, procedures, and retention schedules. (030203)

Knowledge of:

- Organizational mission, vision, goals, and objectives
- IG framework
- Business process improvement concepts and techniques
- Organizational IT requirements
- Stakeholder requirements
- Benchmarking techniques, trends, and methodologies
- Organizational legal and regulatory requirements
- Long-term value of information
- Organizational risk tolerance
- Records coordinator requirements
- End-user requirements
- Organizational contractual and audit obligations
- Organizational legal hold policy and procedures

Skills:

- Research regulations and legal requirements, analyze data, and present findings and recommendations
- Communicate effectively with stakeholders, records coordinators, and end users, orally and in writing
- Incorporate requirements into RIM tools
- Develop training for retention policy, procedures, and schedules
- Develop legal hold policy and procedures with in-house or outside counsel
- Develop the RIM/IG audit component with the internal audit function or outside auditors
- Collaborate with stakeholders to implement policies, procedures, and retention schedules

Manage records retention and disposition in compliance with RIM/IG program policy; legal, regulatory, contractual, and audit requirements; and business needs. (030204)

Knowledge of:

- Disposition methods as defined by policies and procedures for each retention schedule series, security classification, and storage medium
- RIM system tools
- Legal holds and preservation orders
- Life cycles for all information assets
- Legal, regulatory, contractual, audit, and business requirements

Skills:

- Draft policies and procedures
- Communicate appropriately for the task, orally and in writing
- Develop process to attest to organizational systems and practices
- Ensure coordination of team members responsible for all aspects of the retention and disposition process
- Use automated document management, records management, or enterprise content management systems
- Assess records and non-records for disposal status
- Document disposal actions according to RIM/IG procedures
- Select disposal methods and oversee the process
- Audit the program

Manage RIM storage facilities (internal and external) to ensure the security and protection of organizational information assets. (030205)

Knowledge of:

- Contract administration
- Customer relationship management
- Occupational safety
- Records storage and preservation
- Facilities management standards
- Loss prevention
- Project management tools and techniques
- Micrographics and other preservation format types
- Electronic and digital asset management
- Records center standards and guidelines
- Access controls for protected information

Skills:

- Manage employees
- Negotiate with vendors
- Provide customer service
- Implement controls over access to information assets
- Monitor and audit environmental controls and conduct visual inspections
- Prepare reports
- Develop specifications
- Allocate resources

Oversee the operation of the records center in accordance with established policies, standards, and best practices. (030206)

Knowledge of:

- Facilities management
- Fire suppression systems
- Storage environments for film and other media
- Records center standards
- Records management software and data input
- Business requirements
- Reporting and metrics
- Environmental, health, and safety issues
- Records transportation and storage
- Budget management
- Commercial RIM service providers' operational best practices
- Records coordinator and end-user requirements

Skills:

- Manage RIM program human resources Manage vendors and oversee the procurement process
- Manage the records center for information security
- Manage inventory control and records retrieval
- Read, interpret, and report on end-user statistics, destruction statistics, and transfer statistics
- Develop standards and procedures for visitors to the records center
- Review, verify, and approve invoices and billing statements
- Maintain collaborative relationships with vendors and third parties

Establish a process to authorize individuals to access RIM/IG program facilities and repositories by evaluating end users' needs in accordance with policies. (030207)

Knowledge of:

- Organizational security and privacy policies
- Freedom of Information Act and similar laws
- Emergency operating procedures and policies
- Information security and privacy methods and practices
- Risks and potential impacts
- Risk evaluation techniques
- Individual and role-based access models
- Records coordinator role and end-user requirements

Skills:

- Apply compliant legal security and privacy requirements to the program
- Analyze the needs of records coordinators and end users
- Determine and assign levels of security granted and the organizational roles they apply to
- Analyze the needs of the requester to access or borrow the information
- Assess the requester's credibility per organizational policy
- Manage the "rights to access" information assets

Develop and implement training programs on RIM/IG processes in compliance with organizational policies and procedures. (030208)

Knowledge of:

- Organizational training needs
- Risk management concerns, including the security of protected information and the protection of records from unauthorized access
- Human resource training programs and the resources available for new development
- Compliance and internal audit requirements
- Training methodologies and techniques
- Training delivery methods (e.g., web, intranet, networking, classes, phone)
- Organizational RIM/IG policies and procedures
- Records coordinator, end user, and other role-based training requirements
- Training program assessment
- "Train the trainer" methodologies

Skills:

- Present approved methods and their rationale
- Train and mentor records coordinators and end users
- Conduct a needs analysis for training
- Obtain support for organization-wide training
- Integrate Generally Accepted Recordkeeping Principles® into the training content
- Evaluate and implement ongoing improvement strategies and tactics
- Test the effectiveness of training

Review and update RIM/IG policies and procedures. (030209)

Knowledge of:

- Generally Accepted Recordkeeping Principles® and best practices
- Policy formulation and procedure writing techniques
- Continual improvement methodologies
- Legal requirements
- Contractual requirements
- Compliance requirements
- Audit requirements
- Organizational stylebook
- Business-appropriate language

Skills:

- Assess corporate culture and RIM/IG priorities
- Communicate appropriately for the task, orally and in writing
- Apply evolving legal requirements
- Interpret and apply contractual requirements
- Coordinate with the compliance officer
- Coordinate with the internal audit function or outside auditors
- Coordinate with public relations or another "owner" of the organizational stylebook
- Promote cross-functional awareness of IG requirements to records coordinators and IT team

Conduct a regular assessment of the RIM/IG program. (030210)

Knowledge of:

- Auditing standards, principles, and techniques
- Organization's legal and regulatory requirements
- Information risks identification
- Feedback and evaluation mechanisms
- Records coordinator network
- Generally Accepted Recordkeeping Principles® and best practices
- Enterprise content management systems design and reporting
- Customer relationship management
- RIM/IG programs and systems
- Data analysis methods and applications
- IG framework
- Survey techniques

Skills:

- Develop, test, and implement systems
- Develop and report metrics for cost, cycle time, effectiveness, customer satisfaction, and process improvement
- Conduct surveys of stakeholders, records coordinators, and end users
- Evaluate program analyses and present findings to management
- Communicate regularly with the records coordinators and their supervisors
- Initiate and monitor corrective actions
- Establish continuous monitoring and regular evaluation to ensure system integrity
- Contribute to audit reports
- Communicate appropriately for the task, orally and in writing
- Resolve conflicts and challenges

Establish and promote organizational policies and practices to preserve and maintain vital records. (030211)

Knowledge of:

- RIM/IG program policy and practice with respect to the management of vital and historical records
- Data migration software and information architecture design
- Vital records classifications and inventories
- Systems documentation analysis
- System integration and interoperability
- Data mapping/data atlas
- Preservation formats for analog and digital materials
- Project management tools and techniques
- Verification, authenticity, and validation of RIM standards
- Business continuity standards and procedures (i.e., for disaster prevention, response, recovery, and resumption of business)
- Backup systems procedures

Skills:

- Articulate the benefits of preserving and having access to vital records
- Communicate effectively with stakeholders, IT staff, facilities staff, records coordinators, and end users
- Review hardware and software specifications
- Test the systems and disaster scenarios
- Maintain an up-to-date vital records schedule and inventories

Develop an organizational policy and practice for the collection and preservation of archival records. (030212)

Knowledge of:

- Professional archives management theory, practices, and standards (e.g., collections policy and accessioning practices)
- Organizational RIM/IG environment
- Organizational culture, strategies, and priorities
- Organizational and community history
- Wider RIM/IG environment (e.g., legislation, regulation, community expectations)
- History of changes in laws, regulations, and requirements

Skills:

- Communicate appropriately for the task, orally and in writing
- Advocate to maintain electronic and physical archival records and artifacts
- Develop and articulate policies and practices
- Analyze the organization's financial situation with respect to archives management

Delegate RIM/IG responsibilities to ensure the creation, capture, management, preservation, retention, and disposition of comprehensive, reliable, authentic records. (030213)

Knowledge of:

- Professional RIM/IG theory, practices, and standards
- Generally Accepted Recordkeeping Principles® and best practices
- Organizational culture, goals, and priorities
- Organizational business functions
- Work product of the RIM/IG/archives program
- Records coordinator role and network

Skills:

- Evaluate the skill set of RIM/IG staff and records coordinators and assign them duties
- Evaluate the procedures applicable to the work product
- Collaborate with relevant stakeholders when changes have been made to RIM policies
- Advocate for sufficient human, financial, and physical resources
- Audit to ensure completion

Monitor metadata to describe records and to document the preservation process. (030214)

Knowledge of:

- Encoded archival description
- Preservation metadata development and control
- Authenticity, integrity, reliability, and usability
- ISO 23081-1:2006, *Information and documentation – Records management processes – Metadata for records – Part 1: Principles;* ISO 23081-2:2009, *Information and documentation – Records management processes – Metadata for records – Part 2: Conceptual and implementation issues;* and ISO 23081-3:2011, *Information and documentation – Records management processes – Metadata for records – Part 3: Self-assessment method*
- Metadata Encoding and Transmission Standard

Skills:

- Manage electronic data and metadata
- Use archival descriptive techniques, templates, and tools

Design and implement a system classification scheme and taxonomies or controlled vocabularies. (030215)

Knowledge of:

- Role and purpose of taxonomies and controlled vocabularies in electronic content management (ECM) systems
- Taxonomy software and ECM thesaurus capabilities
- Controlled vocabulary development and structure
- Organizational business functions and information assets
- Organizational RIM/IG environment
- Business strategy, policies, and objectives
- Information management system design
- Statutory, regulatory, and contractual requirements

Skills:

- Design a logical classification scheme
- Develop the process and procedure documentation
- Advocate for and articulate the benefits of using controlled vocabularies
- Collaborate with stakeholders, records coordinators, and end users on the implementation and use of classification structures
- Ensure the system classification scheme is compliant with legal and regulatory requirements
- Plan the project implementation strategy and tactics
- Identify the need for changes to metadata
- Communicate appropriately for the task, orally and in writing

Develop and implement a template management program. (030216)

Knowledge of:

- Template design, structure, function, and usage
- IT principles and applications
- Business documentation processes
- Organizational regulatory and legal environments
- Data collection design principles
- Version control practices
- User interface testing and development

Skills:

- Control the creation of templates
- Analyze template usage
- Communicate appropriately for the task, orally and in writing
- Solicit input, establish consensus, and obtain approval from end users
- Develop template guidelines
- Use graphic design applications
- Provide guidance for template design

Lead or assist with a privacy impact assessment. (030217)

Knowledge of:

- Privacy laws and requirements, including multi-jurisdictional requirements
- ISO 29100:2011, *Information Technology - Security Techniques - Privacy Framework*
- Organizational policies for protecting information
- Organizational locations (e.g., systems, repositories, storage areas) that contain and use personally identifiable information (PII)
- Risk assessment processes
- Data mapping

Skills:

- Understand stakeholder needs and requirements
- Articulate the benefits and/or risks of storage technologies
- Align system access controls to their appropriate data types
- Contribute RIM expertise to breach response plans
- Collaborate with SMEs and departments that develop and/or oversee privacy impact assessments

Monitor legal developments that impact RIM practices, and communicate relevant developments to management. (030218)

Knowledge of:

- Organization's e-discovery procedures
- Legal hold process, including notification, preservation, and release
- Legal and regulatory requirements
- Resources for identifying legal developments related to RIM (e.g., NARA, ARMA, American Bar Association)
- Legal retention requirements

Skills:

- Monitor organizational policies and procedures, and communicate the potential RIM impact to the affected areas
- Identify conflicting task instructions and notify management
- Verify appropriateness of authorization
- Communicate appropriately for the task, orally and in writing

Implement, manage, and test the plans to protect organizational vital records and information assets. (030219)

Knowledge of:

- *Vital Records* (ARMA International TR 29-2017) and related practices
- IT applications and processes
- Disaster and recovery planning techniques and practices
- Capabilities of remote access via cloud
- Organizational emergency planning procedures
- Statutes, regulations, and contracts requiring protection of vital records
- Hazards around the organization's primary business location, its recovery site, and the vital records locations
- Capabilities of remote access from hot, warm, or cold sites
- Components of a vital records schedule
- Capabilities of remote locations (e.g., branch offices) to store and provide access to vital records
- Appropriate storage conditions for various types of vital records consistent with media format
- Agreements with vendors storing vital records
- Resource planning for the emergency operations center
- Sources for media conversion
- Proper cataloging and protection methods for vital records

Skills:

- Negotiate contracts with service providers for vital records storage
- Coach emergency teams and end users on how to operate in the event of a disaster
- Coordinate access to vital records after a business interruption
- Confirm that the records in vital records storage are current and accessible
- Operate during emergency conditions
- Evaluate media options
- Lead the business continuity and disaster recovery teams
- Communicate appropriately for the task, orally and in writing

Domain: Risk Management

Risk Management: This domain pertains to the knowledge and skills necessary to proactively mitigate and manage the potential for damage, loss, or unauthorized access to information assets. Two risk management components – risk analysis, which identifies the probabilities that information will be damaged or lost, and risk assessment, which examines known or anticipated risk to information – are key concepts to systematically controlling the level of risk exposure of an organization. Additional risk management components from an operational perspective are business continuity, disaster preparedness and recovery, information privacy and security requirements, and auditing.

Level 3

Collaborate with legal counsel and/or risk management to develop and implement the legal hold process and the resumption of records destruction. (030301)

Knowledge of:

- Laws, regulations, and statutes related to retention and disposition
- Organizational policies and procedures
- Organizational structure and environment
- Risk management, data loss prevention, and mitigation techniques
- Data deletion practices
- Legal hold and release notification and business resumption communication system
- Legal hold release and retention resumption processes
- Organizational workflow and position accountability
- Legacy and orphaned systems in which information assets are managed
- Data storage practices and media
- Advocacy and marketing techniques
- Training methodologies and techniques
- Preservation requirements and procedures
- Secure destruction procedures
- *The Sedona Conference® 2010 Commentary on Legal Holds: The Trigger & The Process*

Skills:

- Provide and improve customer service (internal and external)
- Develop policies and procedures
- Prepare status reports
- Develop and deliver presentations
- Create, maintain, and publish training related to functional procedures for staff
- Communicate effectively with stakeholders, orally and in writing
- Communicate the risk of non-compliance

Develop a RIM assessment program to evaluate compliance for meeting internal and external requirements. (030302)

Knowledge of:

- Auditing principles and techniques
- Relevant organizational operating environment
- Applicable RIM industry compliance requirements
- Organizational compliance requirements and procedures
- Relevant ethical business practices
- Applicable quality control standards
- Organization's legal department and its processes
- IT principles and processes

Skills:

- Evaluate practices to determine any potential gaps
- Communicate effectively with stakeholders, orally and in writing
- Write accurate program components
- Determine the appropriate assessment process
- Apply the relevant legal and regulatory requirements to the business process
- Develop a plan to implement compliance requirements across the organization

Establish and manage access control protocols for RIM systems by following an organized and periodic review model. (030303)

Knowledge of:

- Information security requirements
- Personnel management
- Authority control
- Security requirements related to information
- User authentication methods
- Data classification schemes and classified information-handling procedures
- Organizational privacy policy
- Laws, regulations, and statutes related to privacy
- Privacy data processing and data controller requirements

Skills:

- Use relevant software and hardware
- Use established procedures and standards for information security
- Manage protocols for access to information repositories
- Communicate requirements
- Analyze and assess data
- Document RIM access procedures and standards for information security

Participate in the risk assessment and audit processes related to information assets. (030304)

Knowledge of:

- Risk analysis and assessment
- Auditing principles and techniques
- Organizational structure and overall environment
- RIM program, policy, practices, and procedures
- ISO 27001:2013, *Information technology – Security techniques – Information security management systems – Requirements*

Skills:

- Write audit reports
- Analyze data
- Communicate appropriately for the task, orally and in writing
- Resolve conflicts and solve problems

Develop a security classification framework, policies, and procedures according to RIM/IG best practices and organizational requirements. (030305)

Knowledge of:

- Security classification scheme creation and administration principles and practices
- Security classification requirements of the organization's records
- Information security requirements
- ISO/IEC 27002:2013, *Information technology – Security techniques – Code of practice for information security controls*

Skills:

- Develop a security classification framework
- Communicate appropriately for the task, orally and in writing
- Write policies and procedures

Comply with information privacy classification policy and procedures. (030306)

Knowledge of:

- Privacy requirements of personally identifiable information and protected health information

Skills:

- Identify issues and report them to the compliance officer
- Analyze and practice the applicable privacy requirements

Manage the control of private and proprietary information and the breach notification process. (030307)

Knowledge of:

- Security classification scheme creation and administration principles and practices
- Security classification requirements for organizational records
- Privacy legislation
- Privacy implications from conflicting laws and obligations
- Privacy issues that impact the organization
- ISO/IEC 27002:2013, *Information technology – Security techniques – Code of practice for information security controls*
- Privacy related regulations for all jurisdictions within which the organization conducts business
- Information classification technologies and their capacity to enforce classification schemes for privacy propagation

Skills:

- Communicate appropriately for the task, orally and in writing
- Market the program benefits to stakeholders and functional areas
- Comply with legal department directives on the breach notification process
- Apply the appropriate security classification to information
- Audit the process
- Educate stakeholders about privacy policies and procedures and monitor compliance
- Maintain privacy checklists
- Design and manage the asset inventory in support of privacy impact assessments
- Develop methods for tracking disclosures and offer suggestions for improvement
- Set up and implement a privacy awareness training program

Collaborate with functional groups to develop and maintain a disaster preparedness and business continuity program. (030308)

Knowledge of:

- Organizational emergency planning procedures
- Organizational vital records schedules
- Agreements with vendors and others storing vital records
- Backups and backup strategies and locations
- Organizational structure and overall environment
- Disaster recovery methodologies
- Information protection methods and associated costs
- Business continuity, process, and impact analysis calculations
- Legal and regulatory impacts related to the loss of information assets
- Agreements with vendors performing disaster recovery
- Business units and vendor functions that must be addressed quickly for an effective recovery process

Skills:

- Evaluate the impact on the organization of a disruption to RIM processes
- Communicate the RIM status if there's a business interruption
- Analyze the needs of the organization to support continued operations
- Analyze and communicate the costs associated with the vital records program
- Select vendors capable of recovering various media types
- Co-develop the RIM elements of the organizational business continuity plan (i.e., for disaster prevention, response, recovery, and resumption of business)

Help implement, manage, and test the business continuity plan to protect the organization's mission-critical information assets. (030309)

Knowledge of:

- Business continuity planning and operations principles and best practices (i.e., for disaster prevention, response, recovery, and resumption of business)
- Organizational business continuity plan
- IT applications and processes
- Components of a vital records schedule
- Legal and regulatory requirements
- Agreements with vendors and others storing vital records
- Resource planning for emergency operation center
- Backups strategies and storage locations
- Media conversion
- Vendor relationships required for recovery efforts
- Testing methodologies

Skills:

- Negotiate contracts for recovery services
- Implement a plan to communicate with employees throughout a business interruption
- Coach employees to operate in the event of a disaster
- Coordinate staff activities while recovering from a business interruption
- Hold disaster recovery drills
- Operate in emergency conditions
- Evaluate media options
- Lead teams
- Communicate appropriately for the task, orally and in writing

Establish a vital records program by identifying records and methods of protection to preserve recorded information that is essential to continued operations. (030310)

Knowledge of:
- Organizational structure
- Organizational interdisciplinary interactions
- Industry standards and best practices for vital records programs
- How to maintain the integrity and availability of long-term information assets
- Records vital to the organization

Skills:
- Assess and prioritize the risks associated with the loss of information assets
- Apply the laws and regulations that affect vital records management
- Communicate the vital records analysis and resulting recommendations
- Resolve any departmental disagreements with recommended program
- Analyze the need to support a vital records management program
- Determine the costs associated with the vital records program and develop the budget
- Develop exercises to practice the recovery of vital records
- Document the vital records management program

Establish and implement organizational policies and practices that establish business continuity plans for records. (030311)

Knowledge of:
- Business continuity planning and best practices (i.e., for disaster prevention, response, recovery, and resumption of business)
- Data migration, systems software, and hardware design
- Risk management, loss prevention, and mitigation techniques
- Resources available for emergency operations
- System integration and interoperability
- Data mapping techniques
- Key contacts in an emergency to resume operations in a timely manner
- Project management tools and techniques
- Standards for protection of vital records appropriate to the organization and industry
- Contracts with providers that store and protect vital records
- Organizational structure and functional capabilities of the operational units
- Impact of loss of access to critical information assets
- Roles of operational units that support business continuity
- Verification, authenticity, and validation guidelines
- Team building and communications

Skills:
- Articulate the benefits of preserving and having access to critical information assets
- Communicate appropriately for the task, orally and in writing
- Review hardware and software specifications
- Determine the records needed for business recovery
- Document RIM needs

Establish and implement organizational policies and practices to preserve and maintain vital records. (030312)

Knowledge of:

- RIM program policy and practices for managing vital records
- Data migration, systems software, and hardware design
- Laws, regulations, and statutes requiring the protection of vital records
- Maintaining the integrity and availability of long-term information assets
- System integration and interoperability
- Assessment criteria to determine the scope of vital records
- Data mapping techniques
- Preservation formats for analog and digital materials
- Project management tools and techniques
- Standards for the protection of vital records appropriate to the organization and industry
- Organizational structure and functional capabilities of the operational units
- Impact of loss of access to critical information assets
- Roles of various operational units to support business continuity
- Conversion and migration strategies
- Contracts with providers that store and protect vital records
- Criteria for evaluating the ability of providers to adequately protect vital records
- Verification, authenticity, and validation guidelines

Skills:

- Articulate the benefits of preserving and having access to legacy information assets
- Persuade stakeholders to comply with RIM policies
- Review hardware and software specifications
- Test the systems
- Determine the records needed for business recovery
- Communicate effectively under pressure
- Collaborate with key stakeholders

Identify technology requirements to enable the organization's privacy programs. (030313)

Knowledge of:

- Information security requirements
- Security and privacy requirements related to protected information
- Data classification schemes and classified information-handling procedures
- Organizational privacy policy
- SDLC development steps with a focus on gathering detailed business requirements

Skills:

- Apply appropriate project management methodologies
- Manage stakeholder expectations
- Communicate requirements
- Evaluate and manage vendors
- Ensure records related contractual language is incorporated in all contracts and statements of work
- Communicate requirements to stakeholders

Direct privacy and proprietary information initiatives with an appropriate breach notification process. (030314)

Knowledge of:

- Privacy legislation
- Security classification requirements
- Organizational intellectual property and capital assets
- Organizational privacy policy and obligations
- Privacy protection standards and best practices
- Industry ethics and guidelines
- Information technology protection standards and best practices
- ISO/IEC 27002:2013, *Information Technology – Security techniques – Code of practice for information security controls*

Skills:

- Collaborate with legal staff on the breach notification process
- Perform public relations and damage control
- Create management awareness
- Promulgate privacy policies and procedures
- Coordinate enterprise-wide implementation of privacy impact assessment
- Collaborate on training content for the privacy awareness initiative

Domain: Communications and Marketing

Communications and Marketing: This domain pertains to the knowledge and skills necessary to effectively exchange thoughts, messages, or information by speech, writing, or behavior and to effectively champion the benefits of a RIM program within an organization or to external stakeholders. The domain covers training and education of users about the RIM program. The Communications and Marketing domain is vital to developing successful business relationships to maximize RIM support and compliance, communicate the importance of RIM, and promote the value of RIM principles and best practices.

Level 3

Identify and develop relationships by networking with internal customers to maximize support and accomplish organizational goals outlined in the strategic plan. (030401)

Knowledge of:
- Partners' and stakeholders' goals and objectives
- Organizational strategic plan
- RIM program goals and objectives
- Available resources (e.g., finances, personnel, equipment, intranet, collaboration sites)
- Organizational electronic communications policy

Skills:
- Focus on value-added interactions relevant to the RIM program
- Build credibility and trust within internal and external partnerships
- Recognize and communicate the value of common goals
- Establish and support collaboration between RIM and its partners

Communicate with key stakeholders to ensure the organization understands the interrelationship of records and business processes. (030402)

Knowledge of:
- Investor relations
- Corporate and interpersonal communications
- Return on investment principles
- Organizational dynamics
- Marketing principles
- Institutional behavior
- Organizational structure, mission, vision, and goals

Skills:
- Develop and deliver presentations
- Negotiate with stakeholders and peers
- Speak to individuals and groups
- Market the benefits of RIM

Provide RIM program expertise to promote efficiencies and maintain compliance. (030403)

Knowledge of:

- Generally Accepted Recordkeeping Principles® and best practices
- RIM operations
- Current business processes
- RIM requirements to meet organizational objectives
- Research methodologies and resources to identify trends and issues that might impact the industry

Skills:

- Communicate RIM knowledge to end users
- Market RIM to the organization
- Audit for compliance and make recommendations based on the findings
- Network to communicate the value of RIM
- Research the RIM industry to identify potential improvements to the program
- Review and apply legal regulations and interpret their impacts on RIM
- Evaluate current events for their applicability to RIM
- Educate, train, and routinely communicate the RIM policy to stakeholders and end users

Communicate organizational policies that promote the value of RIM principles and best practices. (030404)

Knowledge of:

- Organizational policies and procedures, including communications programs
- Core business model and organizational structure
- Available tools and media and how to leverage them most effectively
- Effective and persuasive communication techniques
- Target audience

Skills:

- Communicate appropriately for the task, orally and in writing
- Apply RIM principles to the business
- Implement appropriate communication tools

Champion the RIM program to senior management to heighten awareness of RIM as a key business resource. (030405)

Knowledge of:

- Core business values and business drivers
- Ethics and organizational code of conduct
- Issues important to executives
- Organizational culture
- Team building and motivational processes
- Social media strategies

Skills:

- Present oneself effectively
- Navigate the political landscape
- Leverage relationships
- Review and approve social media content
- Communicate appropriately for the task, orally and in writing

Comply with policies and processes for providing appropriate access to organizational information. (030406)

Knowledge of:

- Organizational structure and communication channels
- Organizational protocols for release of information
- Public relations principles
- Communication techniques
- Organizational policies and risk protocol
- Current and potential stakeholders and customers

Skills:

- Communicate the value of applying best practices
- Network with peers to gather ideas and knowledge
- Evaluate upcoming projects for opportunities for RIM involvement

Communicate RIM activities to stakeholders to increase awareness of RIM's importance to the organization. (030407)

Knowledge of:

- Organizational structure and communication channels
- Public relations principles
- Communication techniques
- Marketing the RIM program
- Current and potential stakeholders and customers
- Organizational goals and objectives
- RIM principles and best practices
- Social media terminology

Skills:

- Communicate RIM benefits to stakeholders and end users
- Communicate the value of applying RIM best practices
- Network with peers to gather ideas and knowledge
- Track the results of social media campaigns
- Evaluate upcoming projects for opportunities for RIM involvement
- Develop and deliver presentations using various media for target audiences

Domain: Information Technology

Information Technology: This domain pertains to the knowledge and skills necessary at the middle management level to develop, maintain, and use information processing systems, software applications, and supporting hardware and networks for the processing and distribution of data. Examples of information technology tasks in this context include the RIM software application selection process, reprographics and imaging equipment, establishing requirements for IT related to managing electronic repositories, and the identification of emerging technologies as they may impact one or more business units and / or business processes that cross functional boundaries.

Level 3

Identify emerging trends and technologies to manage information assets. (030501)

Knowledge of:

- Current and emerging trends and technologies, including cloud services, mobile, and Internet of Things
- Enterprise systems and related compatibility
- Legal, regulatory, and business requirements, including complying with relevant software and hardware licensing agreements
- Legacy operating systems
- Business techniques and measurement tools
- Applications for information management
- Requirements for security and information preservation
- Privacy issues for information protection, including data processing and controlling roles
- Data storage practices and media
- Budgeting for technology and its support
- RIM principles and best practices
- Social media tools and platforms
- Change management tools and techniques

Skills:

- Select emerging technology solutions
- Match resources to the available solutions
- Conduct interviews and collect information
- Identify trends
- Develop and implement decision-making tools
- Specify technical functionality requirements
- Manage social media content for an improved digital experience
- Identify RIM compliance gaps for emerging technologies
- Plan and apply change management techniques when new IT tools are implemented
- Draft privacy and security policies and procedures for bring your own device and bring your own cloud

Establish objectives and collaborate with IT to meet the requirements for managing repositories and other information assets. (030502)

Knowledge of:

- Current IT systems and potential improvements
- IT department's technology strategy
- How legacy systems interface with their replacements
- Archival storage tools and technologies
- Data mapping tools and technologies
- Media selection tools and technologies
- Migration methodologies and strategy
- Enterprise systems and related compatibility
- Database options for RIM solutions
- Data conversion techniques
- Data storage practices and media
- Interviewing skills and techniques
- IT practices and policies for project management, including the project management life cycle
- RIM requirements for maintaining reliable and authentic records
- Change management tools and techniques
- Procurement of RIM tools, technologies, and services
- Integration methods for new repositories and data systems

Skills:

- Collect information from relevant stakeholders
- Choose appropriate technology solutions
- Document objectives for the use of technology in managing information assets
- Communicate RIM, legal, regulatory, and privacy requirements to IT
- Identify gaps in the functional requirements for the current and future state
- Develop service level agreements to measure and manage RIM performance
- Identify and develop metrics for the efficacy of social media content
- Manage RIM repositories for unstructured content
- Collaborate with the procurement team
- Integrate the business, legal, and compliance requirements into IT requirements for procurement documents

Collaborate with IT to define and address the incorporation of lifecycle management requirements into the design of information management systems. (030503)

Knowledge of:

- Metadata standards
- IT practices
- Current and emerging RIM technologies
- Stakeholder requirements
- Retention schedule development, implementation, and monitoring, including mapping retention as a part of system configuration
- Policies and procedures for managing sensitive, restricted, and private information
- RIM preservation procedures, practices, and techniques
- System documentation requirements
- Cloud and on-premises storage risks and benefits
- Access control and version management

Skills:

- Negotiate and communicate appropriately for the task, orally and in writing
- Select RIM and business software applications
- Specify business and technical functionality requirements
- Define proof of concept solutions requirements to assess the ability to meet RIM requirements
- Develop collaboratively with IT the RIM policies and procedures framework
- Define and analyze the requirements for information lifecycle management for cloud, on-premises, or hybrid storage

Collaborate with IT to implement RIM requirements during the operation, maintenance, and close-out phases of the information management system lifecycle.
(030504)

Knowledge of:

- System capabilities as designed
- Recordkeeping requirements
- System testing procedures
- System documentation requirements
- IT practices and policies
- Current and emerging RIM technologies
- Stakeholder requirements
- Retention schedule implementation and monitoring
- RIM preservation procedures, practices, and techniques
- Archival storage solutions as part of lifecycle management
- Data mapping
- Data storage practices and media selection
- Data migration methods and requirements
- RIM requirements for maintaining reliable and authentic records
- Compliant project close-out processes for decommissioning systems

Skills:

- Communicate persuasively with stakeholders
- Evaluate system performance against requirements
- Communicate appropriately for the task, orally and in writing
- Choose appropriate technology solutions
- Communicate RIM requirements and regulatory requirements to IT
- Conduct proof of concept review and provide feedback
- Assess the impacts of change for the lines of business
- Assess the training needs for various audiences
- Review knowledge transfer initiatives
- Audit the process

Domain: Leadership

Leadership: This domain pertains to the knowledge and skills necessary to increase RIM awareness and motivate groups of people toward the achievement of the RIM program goals within the context of the organization's overall goals. Effective leaders must positively influence others by using leadership skills such as guiding, motivating, mentoring, and promoting continuing education and learning; interpersonal skills such as empathy and sensitivity; creative thinking skills such as brainstorming and thinking untraditionally; and change management skills such as trust building and networking.

Level 3

Communicate the ways in which RIM projects support organizational goals and objectives. (030601)

Knowledge of:

- Organizational structure, business strategy, policies, and objectives
- RIM program goals
- Industry trends and current events
- Consensus building
- Public relations principles
- Communication techniques
- Current and potential stakeholders and customers and their priorities

Skills:

- Communicate appropriately for the task, orally and in writing
- Develop and deliver presentations using various media for target audiences
- Analyze organizational processes to identify the potential impact of improved information management
- Present and defend viable recommendations from data collection, research, and analysis

Foster effectiveness during changes in tasks, work environment, or conditions affecting the organization. (030602)

Knowledge of:

- Organizational change
- Organizational environment and culture
- Organizational policies and procedures
- Conflict management styles and strategies

Skills:

- Adapt behavior and work methods to respond positively to change
- Communicate appropriately for the task, orally and in writing
- Cooperate and collaborate during change
- Inspire and guide others toward goal accomplishments
- Manage stressful situations

Manage and mediate conflict. (030603)

Knowledge of:

- Effects of conflict
- Cross-cultural considerations in dealing with conflict
- Conflict management styles and strategies
- Personality types
- Motivational theories
- Mediation techniques

Skills:

- Assess and manage interpersonal conflict in the RIM program
- Listen to facilitate understanding and prevent conflict
- Demonstrate and identify different courses of action
- Demonstrate honesty and act according to ethical principles
- Foster cooperative working relationships
- Exercise good judgment by making well-informed decisions
- Negotiate win/win solutions
- Adjust rapidly to new situations warranting attention and resolution

Empower others through leadership and training to maximize RIM professionals' potential and create a positive work environment. (030604)

Knowledge of:

- Technical and business skills
- Personal strengths and weaknesses
- Career path development
- Training methodologies and techniques
- Group and interpersonal dynamics
- Coaching and mentoring techniques
- Performance management
- Performance objectives

Skills:

- Model RIM values
- Deliver on commitments
- Maintain confidentiality
- Demonstrate honesty and act according to ethical principles
- Apply innovative solutions to make organizational improvements
- Foster an environment that encourages creative thinking and innovation
- Identify and adjust rapidly to new situations warranting attention and resolution
- Lead and manage an inclusive workplace that maximizes the talents of each person to achieve RIM goals
- Seek feedback and opportunities to master new skills
- Recognize employee achievement
- Exercise good judgment by making well-informed decisions

Foster behaviors to achieve organizational goals. (030605)

Knowledge of:

- Goal setting
- Team-building principles
- Group and interpersonal dynamics
- Organizational policies and procedures
- Organizational goals
- Coaching and mentoring techniques
- Performance management
- Performance objectives

Skills:

- Develop cooperative working relationships
- Treat customers and co-workers with dignity, respect, and fairness
- Set specific, measurable, achievable, realistic, and timely (SMART) objectives
- Respect others' ideas and opinions
- Demonstrate commitment, team spirit, and trust
- Change behavior in response to constructive criticism
- Demonstrate quality work
- Demonstrate honesty and act according to ethical principles
- Assign responsibility for delivering on commitments
- Create a work environment that encourages innovation
- Lead and manage to maximize the talents of each person to achieve goals
- Recognize, identify, and resolve team behaviors that warrant special attention
- Identify situations that warrant management attention
- Recognize employee achievement

Evaluate RIM staff career development plans through periodic reviews, and provide mentoring to improve staff effectiveness and skills. (030606)

Knowledge of:

- Basic human resource management principles
- Management communication principles
- Interpersonal communication principles
- Career path development
- Generally Accepted Recordkeeping Principles® and best practices
- Feedback and evaluation mechanisms
- Professional codes of conduct

Skills:

- Communicate appropriately for the task, orally and in writing
- Motivate and coach
- Set realistic goals
- Evaluate personnel development

Level 4: This level RIM practitioner is at the executive level, making strategic decisions, partnering with organizational executive management, and giving enterprise direction to RIM program staff and program users. Practitioners at this level frequently hold advanced degrees and appropriate certifications. For personal growth, continuing education focuses on business strategy, change management, business policies, leading teams, and collaborations and partnerships.

Domain: Business Functions

Business Functions: This domain pertains to the knowledge and skills necessary to administer, implement, or maintain the non-RIM specific functions an organization performs, or needs to perform, to achieve its objectives. Examples of business functions include the supervision of RIM staff, budgeting, providing customer service, identifying and mapping work processes, providing input to management, and strategic planning.

Level 4

Develop a strategic plan for a RIM program using best practice methodologies to achieve long-range organizational goals. (040101)

Knowledge of:

- Strategic planning methodologies
- RIM program and best practice components
- Industry-specific guidelines and regulations
- Consulting methodologies, including data collection, analysis, and diagnosis
- System analysis procedures
- Communication strategies
- Business process and organizational analysis
- Organizational policies, plans, missions, visions, and values

Skills:

- Identify organizational goals
- Assess current business practices (environmental scan)
- Direct the management of the current program
- Evaluate baseline activity levels
- Identify risks
- Define the scope of the RIM program (e.g., business lines, organization sites, international program)
- Define RIM goals and objectives
- Forecast near-future business conditions
- Target reports toward specific audiences
- Obtain peer and executive management support
- Negotiate support from stakeholders and decision makers

Direct the management of the RIM program to meet business objectives and ensure customer service. (040102)

Knowledge of:

- Organizational goals and objectives
- Management and supervisory principles
- RIM program goals, objectives, and capabilities
- Generally Accepted Recordkeeping Principles® and advanced RIM best practices
- Organizational funding priorities and budgeting
- Human resource management principles
- Change management principles
- Customer relationship management
- Legal and regulatory requirements

Skills:

- Adapt change management principles to the organization
- Communicate appropriately for the task, orally and in writing
- Solve problems
- Adjust RIM priorities to remain consistent with organizational changes
- Identify program gaps and make recommendations for program improvement
- Lead and motivate staff
- Resolve conflict

Evaluate and approve changes to the RIM program by reviewing feasibility studies and business cases and by monitoring trends. (040103)

Knowledge of:

- Value of the RIM program in satisfying organizational objectives
- RIM program goals, objectives, principles, and capabilities
- Organizational cost/benefit analysis methods and metrics
- Organizational business case and process requirements
- Technological trends relevant to the RIM program objectives
- RIM profession and its principles and practices

Skills:

- Make strategic decisions for the RIM program
- Determine and negotiate RIM costs, timelines, and staffing levels
- Analyze the benefits of business strategies
- Track and assess emerging trends
- Analyze findings and apply them to the RIM program

Provide program and project information to executive management and stakeholders. (040104)

Knowledge of:

- Organizational goals and objectives
- Components of a RIM program that follows best practices
- Program and project planning
- Program and project analysis and reporting
- Advanced communication techniques
- Organizational analysis

Skills:

- Compile informational reports
- Identify performance indicators
- Organize, analyze, and interpret information
- Collaborate with stakeholders
- Report progress
- Communicate appropriately for the task, orally and in writing

Review, recommend, and revise organizational business policies to comply with technology, legal, and RIM requirements. (040105)

Knowledge of:

- RIM program strategy and goals
- RIM industry standards and best practices
- Organizational human resource policies
- IT security standards
- IT infrastructure design and policies
- Data structure and information flow
- Metadata business rules
- Media used to store data
- Legal and regulatory requirements, including applicable privacy requirements
- Business operations, policies, and requirements

Skills:

- Communicate appropriately for the task, orally and in writing
- Document organizational business policies
- Review IM and IT processes that are applicable to RIM
- Analyze and interpret business, legal, and RIM requirements

Attain new insights, question conventional **RIM** approaches, and implement innovative programs and processes for using information assets. (040106)

Knowledge of:

- Change management
- RIM principles, corporate culture, organizational goals, and business functions
- RIM industry trends
- Organizational legal and regulatory environments

Skills:

- Identify high-level program requirements
- Identify critical success factors
- Develop baseline activity levels
- Develop performance measure guidelines and metrics
- Identify required resources
- Identify costs and benefits
- Develop budgets
- Identify dependencies and constraints
- Develop and manage business plans
- Define problems and develop solutions
- Serve as a catalyst and change agent
- Break down the long-term vision into achievable projects

Comment on draft legislation, regulations, and statutes as required. (040107)

Knowledge of:

- Applicable legislative, regulatory, political processes
- Legal and regulatory requirements
- Current RIM environment
- RIM program strategy and goals
- Strategic planning techniques and methodology
- RIM best practices and standards
- Advocacy and outreach

Skills:

- Provide leadership
- Gauge political and cultural climates
- Influence constituents

Define current and future RIM program staffing requirements. (040108)

Knowledge of:

- Impact of organizational processes on RIM
- RIM program goals and objectives
- Staff productivity methodologies
- Process evaluation and assessment
- Time-and-motion study techniques and sciences
- Generally Accepted Recordkeeping Principles®
- Human behavior and relevant workplace productivity

Skills:

- Develop, monitor, and report on task analyses
- Develop the components of a best practice RIM program
- Develop and hire for staff positions
- Define roles, responsibilities, and needed competencies
- Make long-range forecasts
- Manage resources
- Develop budgets
- Measure performance
- Identify and encourage diverse skill sets in the RIM work force
- Develop succession plans
- Create job descriptions
- Assess and justify staffing requirements

Evaluate, authorize, and acquire organizational resources to administer the RIM program. (040109)

Knowledge of:

- Generally Accepted Recordkeeping Principles®
- Financial analysis, including preparation of budgets and allocation and authorization of expenditures
- Auditing principles, techniques, and methodologies
- Contract administration
- Business financial strategies and objectives
- Resource allocation and optimization

Skills:

- Analyze outsourcing trends and opportunities
- Develop strategic sources for purchasing resources
- Analyze return on investment
- Analyze financial budget variances
- Develop cost/benefit analyses and results
- Develop feasibility studies and outcomes
- Manage vendor relationships, performance, and costs

Demonstrate the value of the RIM program to acquire organizational resources. (040110)

Knowledge of:

- Organizational goals and objectives
- Organizational structure
- Current and future value of the RIM program to the organization
- Internal and external public relations and marketing practices
- Asset allocation and funding priorities

Skills:

- Communicate the RIM program's value
- Market the RIM program
- Analyze the value of the RIM program
- Communicate appropriately for the task, orally and in writing, even when data is limited or indicates unpleasant consequences
- Perceive the impact and implications of decisions
- Build consensus through compromise

Allocate resources to ensure the efficient and effective implementation of RIM program requirements. (040111)

Knowledge of:

- Organizational goals and objectives
- Organizational funding priorities
- Organizational structure
- Human resource principles
- Productivity guidelines, measurements, and metrics
- Organizational process for determining return on investment
- RIM program goals, objectives, and capabilities
- Financial analysis
- Organizational financial strategies and objectives
- Resource allocation and optimization
- Service level agreements, service valuations, and pricing formulas

Skills:

- Assess the value of the RIM program in the context of the organization's goals
- Analyze budget variances
- Develop accurate cost/benefit analyses and results
- Conduct feasibility studies
- Finalize, justify, and administer the budget process with the RIM department
- Oversee procurement and contracting resources
- Periodically review allocations and adjust them as needed

Domain: RIM/IG Practices

RIM/IG Practices: This domain pertains to the knowledge and skills required to systematically manage information assets from creation or receipt through processing, distributing, sharing, using, accessing, organizing, storing and retrieving, and disposing of them. Information is a vital organizational asset, and organizations depend on accurate, complete, and readily available information to assist in making decisions; providing litigation support; improving organizational efficiency; documenting compliance with legislative, regulatory, contractual, and audit requirements; and providing historical reference.

Level 4

Review the RIM/IG program effectiveness by setting benchmarks, evaluating program performance, and reallocating resources. (040201)

Knowledge of:

- RIM/IG program output and results
- RIM/IG program strategy, objectives, principles, and requirements
- Generally Accepted Recordkeeping Principles® and best practices
- Corporate culture, strategies, tactics, and objectives (at an expert level)
- ISO 15489-1: 2016 *Information and documentation – Records management – Concepts and principles*
- Organizational funding priorities and where the RIM/IG program fits into that structure
- Legal hold requirements
- RIM/IG program productivity levels and effectiveness
- RIM/IG benchmarking principles and practices
- Auditing principles, techniques, and methodologies

Skills:

- Communicate appropriately for the task, orally and in writing
- Define metrics to track return on investment, effectiveness, efficiency, and productivity
- Assess if business and end-user requirements are being met
- Identify relevant dependencies and constraints
- Assess the credibility and accuracy of achieving performance metrics
- Prioritize asset allocation effectively and efficiently
- Measure RIM/IG performance and set targets for improvement

Identify legal developments with RIM implications in order to provide the strategic direction for the organization. (040202)

Knowledge of:

- Organizational e-discovery procedures
- New and developing national and international laws and legal requirements that have implications for RIM
- Recent legal decisions that affect RIM
- Legal forms and templates
- Resources for identifying RIM-related legal developments
- Change management

Skills:

- Assess national and international legal requirements and developments for their impact on RIM
- Research and analyze relevant data
- Communicate appropriately for the task, orally and in writing
- Develop policy
- Manage organizational change effectively

Develop RIM/IG policies and procedures by reviewing and analyzing recordkeeping methodologies and requirements consistent with industry best practices. (040203)

Knowledge of:

- Current RIM/IG theory and best practices
- Organizational RIM/IG program charter, policies, procedures, and retention schedules
- Procedure-writing methodology and practices
- Organization's statutory, regulatory, and contractual environment
- Upper management and the RIM/IG steering committee's expectations for RIM

Skills:

- Research and analyze relevant data
- Communicate appropriately for the task, orally and in writing
- Identify changes in legal, industry, and contractual requirements
- Persuade RIM/IG stakeholders and end users
- Develop and implement RIM/IG-compliant policy, procedures, and retention schedule
- Negotiate budget and resources for RIM/IG programs
- Advocate for the RIM/IG program with organizational management
- Collaborate with general counsel to influence organizational policies and procedures affected by legal, privacy, and regulatory issues

Collaborate with functional groups and contractors to develop, implement, and maintain business continuity programs. (040204)

Knowledge of:

- Organizational emergency planning policies and procedures
- Organizational vital records schedules and inventories
- Agreements with vendors and others storing vital records
- Backup policies, strategies, and storage locations
- Organizational structure and overall environment
- Protection methods and associated costs
- Business continuity, process, and impact analysis methodologies
- Risk analysis methodologies
- Legal and regulatory impacts related to the loss of information or records
- Agreements with vendors who provide disaster recovery
- Protection of recorded information that is essential to continuing operations
- Disaster recovery methodologies and vendor relationships required for recovery efforts
- Organizational disaster recovery plan
- Negotiation of contracts for services with outsource service provider firms for recovery assistance
- Business recovery operations
- Requirements to re-establish operations after a disaster
- Testing methodologies

Skills:

- Evaluate the necessary actions if a business interruption impacts RIM/IG
- Communicate the RIM/IG status following a business interruption
- Analyze the needs of the organization to support continued operations
- Analyze and communicate the costs associated with the vital records program
- Select vendors capable of recovering various media types
- Develop elements of organizational business continuity plan and program (i.e., for disaster prevention, response, recovery, and resumption of business)
- Implement a plan to communicate with emergency response teams and employees during and after a business interruption
- Coach emergency response teams and employees on how to operate in the event of a disaster
- Coordinate staff activities in recovering from a business interruption
- Hold disaster recovery drills
- Lead the business continuity and disaster recovery teams
- Communicate appropriately for the task, orally and in writing

Domain: Risk Management

Risk Management: This domain pertains to the knowledge and skills necessary to proactively mitigate and manage the potential for damage, loss, or unauthorized access to information assets. Two risk management components—risk analysis, which identifies the probabilities that information will be damaged or lost, and risk assessment, which examines known or anticipated risk to information—are key concepts to systematically controlling the level of risk exposure of an organization. Additional risk management components from an operational perspective are business continuity, disaster preparedness and recovery, information privacy and security requirements, and auditing.

Level 4

Implement a strategy to identify and mitigate potential RIM risks. (040301)

Knowledge of:

- Organizational business, legal, and regulatory requirements
- Consent requirements for external marketing to ensure compliance with anti-spam statutes in all applicable legal jurisdictions
- Organizational business plans, goals, and objectives
- RIM program goals, objectives, capabilities, and principles
- Compliance requirements for intellectual property law, copyright, trademarks, and patents
- Merger, acquisition, and divestiture impacts
- Internal and external processes and associated RIM-related vulnerabilities

Skills:

- Forecast RIM management risks
- Articulate and communicate risks
- Evaluate and mitigate organizational risks and follow due diligence procedures
- Identify, develop, and implement solutions
- Assess the RIM programs of organizations that are targeted for acquisition
- Document RIM risk strategies

Develop and implement RIM compliance strategies and enforce corrective actions. (040302)

Knowledge of:

- Organizational business, legal, and regulatory requirements
- Organizational business plans, goals, and objectives
- RIM program goals, objectives, capabilities, and principles
- Project management
- IT security standards
- IT infrastructure design and policies
- Data structure and information flow
- Metadata business rules
- Gap analysis methodology
- Corrective action planning
- Classification, retention, disposition, and destruction of all information and media
- Media used to store data
- Organizational compliance management strategies

Skills:

- Collaborate with IT to achieve RIM principles
- Partner with senior management on compliance enforcement processes
- Communicate appropriately for the task, orally and in writing
- Review RIM and IT procedures used throughout the organization
- Assess the RIM program relevant to business operations, legal, and RIM requirements
- Collect and assess the metrics for non-compliance
- Perform a strategic analysis of business, technology, and RIM industries and appropriate applications
- Apply business process re-engineering skills, techniques, and methodologies
- Provide leadership
- Define and implement corrective actions

Respond to requests for compliance information to assist in organizational governance.
(040303)

Knowledge of:

- Legal and regulatory requirements
- Organizational governance structure
- Metrics to assess RIM program performance
- Compliance reporting

Skills:

- Analyze and interpret compliance requirements
- Present options for decision-making
- Identify, evaluate, and present risks associated with non-compliance
- Communicate appropriately for the task, orally and in writing

Partner with legal counsel to design, develop, and deploy litigation readiness protocols, including for legal holds and for the resumption of records disposition. (040304)

Knowledge of:

- Laws, regulations, and statutes related to retention and disposition
- Risk management, loss prevention, and mitigation techniques
- Organizational security and privacy policy and procedures
- Organizational structure, infrastructure, workflow, and position accountability
- Data storage practices and media
- Legacy, orphaned, and inactive systems where information assets are managed
- Legal hold notification and business resumption communication systems
- Advocacy and marketing techniques
- Legal hold processes that include notification, preservation, and release
- Resumption of information asset disposition processes
- Audit procedures for legal hold processes
- Data map development

Skills:

- Provide internal and external customer service
- Write policies and procedures for a wide audience
- Communicate appropriately for the task, orally and in writing
- Identify the costs for non-compliance and benefits of compliance
- Identify the required resources for developing, deploying, and maintaining litigation readiness protocols
- Create and document training for all levels of staff
- Develop audit techniques and processes to monitor and spot check the legal hold process

Collaborate with the leaders of functional groups to plan, develop, and provide support for a RIM focus within the business continuity program. (040305)

Knowledge of:

- Business continuity procedures, best practices, systems, and tools (i.e., for disaster prevention, response, recovery, and resumption of business)
- Organizational vital records requirements
- Organizational structure and environment
- Vendor relationships required for business continuity
- Information protection methods and their costs
- Business continuity impact analysis calculations
- Protection of information assets essential to business continuity
- Legal and regulatory penalties due to the loss of information assets
- Available resources (e.g., finances, personnel, equipment)
- Agreements with business continuity vendors

Skills:

- Prepare a business continuity plan
- Evaluate the impact of a business disruption on RIM processes
- Analyze the needs of the organization to support business continuity
- Analyze and communicate the costs associated with the vital records program
- Develop elements of organizational business continuity
- Influence other business unit leaders within the organization
- Communicate the necessity of developing a business continuity program
- Communicate the impact of a business disruption on RIM processes
- Test the RIM components of the business continuity plan and adjust them as needed
- Obtain financial support for the vital records program
- Communicate appropriately for the task, orally and in writing

Manage, evaluate, and maintain the RIM business continuity program. (040306)

Knowledge of:

- Organizational business continuity procedures (i.e., for disaster prevention, response, recovery, and resumption of business)
- Organizational vital records requirements
- Organizational structure and environment
- Business continuity systems and tools
- Protection methods and associated costs
- Legal and regulatory requirements related to the loss of information assets
- Protection of information assets essential to the continued operations of the organization
- Business continuity planning, testing, and best practices
- Available resources (e.g., finances, personnel, equipment)

Skills:

- Prepare a business continuity plan
- Evaluate the impact of a business disruption on RIM processes
- Communicate the impact of a business disruption on RIM
- Obtain financial support for the costs associated with the vital records program
- Communicate appropriately for the task, orally and in writing
- Lead RIM staff during disaster recovery
- Negotiate agreements with vendors that store vital records

Partner with C-level IT management and senior business leaders to identify and mitigate privacy risks for the organization's information. (040307)

Knowledge of:

- Privacy legislation
- Privacy standards and best practices
- IT best practices for identifying private data
- Organizational privacy policy
- Data mapping techniques

Skills:

- Develop a business case for IT improvements to mitigate information privacy risks
- Create management awareness and support of IT
- Promote privacy policies and procedures
- Identify and define current and potential problems and develop solutions

Direct privacy and proprietary information initiatives with a breach notification process. (040308)

Knowledge of:

- Privacy legislation
- Security classification requirements
- Organizational intellectual property and capital assets
- Organizational privacy policy
- Information privacy standards and best practices (e.g., ISO/IEC 27002:2013, *Information Technology – Security techniques – Code of practice for information security controls*)
- Industry ethics and guidelines
- IT protection standards and best practices

Skills:

- Collaborate with legal staff on developing and implementing the breach notification process
- Perform public relations and damage control
- Create management awareness
- Promote privacy policies and procedures
- Coordinate enterprise-wide implementation of a privacy impact assessment
- Collaborate on identifying and developing content for privacy awareness training
- Identify and define current and potential problems and develop solutions

Domain: Communications and Marketing

Communications and Marketing: This domain pertains to the knowledge and skills necessary to effectively exchange thoughts, messages, or information by speech, writing, or behavior and to effectively champion the benefits of a RIM program within an organization or to external stakeholders. The domain covers training and education of users about the RIM program. The Communications and Marketing domain is vital to developing successful business relationships to maximize RIM support and compliance, communicate the importance of RIM, and promote the value of RIM principles and best practices.

Level 4

Collaborate with stakeholders in developing a communications strategy to achieve awareness and integration of the RIM program. (040401)

Knowledge of:

- Organizational goals and objectives
- Organizational structure
- Strategic planning techniques and methodologies
- Communication tools
- RIM program goals, objectives, principles, and requirements

Skills:

- Develop sales and marketing strategies for the RIM program
- Build internal and external coalitions
- Develop and implement team-building techniques
- Collaborate with subject matter experts to deliver complementary messages
- Align the RIM program with the organization's goals and strategic direction
- Communicate appropriately for the task, orally and in writing

Communicate RIM program requirements and goals through education and relationships to reinforce compliance, best practices, and industry standards. (040402)

Knowledge of:

- RIM program strategy and goals
- RIM standards and best practices
- Human resource policies (e.g., job descriptions and performance appraisals)
- IT policies, infrastructure, and security standards
- Data structure and information flow
- Metadata business rules
- Classification, retention, and disposition of information and media
- Types and methods of information storage
- Information privacy and data-handling policies and procedures

Skills:

- Communicate appropriately for the task, orally and in writing
- Influence all levels of the organization and develop partnerships
- Solve problems
- Review RIM and applicable IT activities to optimize use of technology in meeting compliance requirements
- Implement and evaluate training
- Collaborate with subject matter experts to deliver complementary messages

Establish and maintain collaborative relationships through participation in RIM-related associations. (040403)

Knowledge of:

- RIM program strategies, goals, and opportunities
- RIM standards and best practices
- IT as it relates to RIM
- RIM profession and technology trends

Skills:

- Communicate with IT staff about relevant RIM technologies
- Communicate with end users, vendors, internal customers, and other stakeholders
- Influence stakeholders
- Identify networking opportunities
- Collaborate across boundaries

Domain: Information Technology

Information Technology: This domain pertains to the knowledge and skills at the executive level necessary to develop, maintain, and use information processing systems, software applications, and supporting hardware and networks for the processing and distribution of data. Along with the examples above, this level includes promoting transparency, accountability, collaboration and RIM policies across the organization and with an enterprise perspective.

Level 4

Establish RIM program methodologies for managing information assets in electronic and digital formats. (040501)

Knowledge of:

- Standards for information authenticity
- Digital library standards for persistent access
- Information life cycle management best practices
- E-mail management methodologies
- Website content management methodologies
- Information conversion and migration strategies
- Imaging standards to digitize paper and analog media
- Total cost of ownership (TCO) methodologies
- RIM quality assurance frameworks

Skills:

- Calculate information storage needs
- Develop and communicate policy
- Evaluate applicable hardware and software
- Allocate resources as part of IT strategic planning
- Develop strategies for RIM awareness
- Develop a change management strategy for information repositories affected by RIM system changes
- Develop strategies for updating RIM policies, information architecture, taxonomies, files plans, etc.
- Communicate RIM initiatives to management and peers to obtain implementation support at all levels
- Lead cross-functional teams to perform TCO analysis and recommendations
- Analyze and assess quality frameworks for the enterprise
- Apply archival resource keys, digital object identifiers, and persistent uniform resource locators to the digital library content

Partner with IT to develop best practices and procedures for managing electronic information repositories. (040502)

Knowledge of:

- Relevant standards for digital preservation
- Conversion and migration strategies
- Electronic records management theory
- Legacy systems
- Requirements for access to data
- Trends in electronic media
- Information storage practices and principles
- Archival storage architectures and standards, including tiered storage
- Data mapping
- Media selection
- Information security requirements
- Data usage principles
- Advocacy and outreach to increase RIM awareness
- Business continuity plans (i.e., for disaster prevention, response, recovery, and resumption of business)
- Stakeholder management and relationship building with business and IT
- Privacy requirements

Skills:

- Collaborate with IT
- Communicate appropriately for the task, orally and in writing
- Evaluate enterprise legacy data
- Solve problems stemming from legacy data
- Consult with stakeholders to develop business continuity strategies
- Partner with business and IT to understand the impact of business disruptions on information repositories
- Collaborate to develop information architectures and their standards
- Lead cross-functional teams and quality enhancement conversations related to IG
- Provide ongoing support and governance to internal stakeholders
- Assess the current situation

Research RIM-related emerging technologies and business trends to assess their applicability to the organization at the enterprise level. (040503)

Knowledge of:

- Management principles, techniques, theories, and practices
- Current and emerging technologies and trends at the enterprise level
- Technological needs of the organization
- Organizations involved in relevant research and development
- Enterprise architecture and its cloud, on-premises, or hybrid RIM solution options
- Organizational use of social media and its curation
- Business architecture in the context of RIM technologies
- Monetization of information assets, especially digital assets
- Information management maturity models for quality and service delivery, including support models
- Digital user experience management to enhance knowledge management and collaboration
- Business analytics and data visualization for business intelligence solutions

Skills:

- Determine the impact of implementing new RIM-related technologies
- Analyze, assess, and champion the benefits of new technology for RIM and the organization
- Communicate to IT the RIM nomenclature when assessing technologies
- Advise stakeholders of the impact of new technologies on RIM
- Analyze the options for RIM-related enterprise architecture
- Develop a solution roadmap to incorporate new technologies
- Consult with business stakeholders to understand and explain the pros and cons of configuring RIM tools
- Explain the differences between IG and digital governance to business users in the context of privacy, security, data in structured databases, reports from structured databases, etc.
- Explain to IT the differences between IG and data governance from a RIM perspective
- Analyze information maturity models
- Develop a framework to integrate the creation, sharing, and use of information and knowledge
- Identify effective ways to use information to support decision-making

Domain: Leadership

Leadership: This domain pertains to the knowledge and skills necessary to increase RIM awareness and motivate groups of people toward the achievement of the RIM program goals within the context of the organization's overall goals. Effective leaders must positively influence others by using leadership skills such as guiding, motivating, mentoring, and promoting continuing education and learning; interpersonal skills such as empathy and sensitivity; creative thinking skills such as brainstorming and thinking untraditionally; and change management skills such as trust building and networking.

Level 4

Provide leadership and strategic direction to successfully operate the enterprise-wide RIM program. (040601)

Knowledge of:

- Enterprise content management
- Electronic records management
- Information technology
- Information security and privacy
- RIM-related legislation
- Vendor relationships
- Project management
- Customer relationship management
- Political influences and seats of power
- Knowledge management
- Strategic planning
- Financial planning and budgeting
- Business values and ethical conduct
- Auditing principles, techniques, and methodologies

Skills:

- Provide leadership
- Analyze RIM program strengths, weaknesses, opportunities, threats (SWOT)
- Adapt to new information or changing conditions

Sponsor projects and programs by reviewing proposals and recommending ways to advance organizational goals and objectives. (040602)

Knowledge of:

- Components of a successful proposal
- Analytical review process for preparing proposals and making recommendations for adoption
- Systems for proposing project for funding and adoption
- Cost/benefit analysis techniques
- Business climate and timing for the promotion of projects

Skills:

- Sell ideas to senior management for implementation
- Negotiate with managers for project support
- Perform project management
- Identify sources of funding and project support
- Present conceptual projects for adoption by stakeholders
- Select staff to manage projects
- Write project proposals
- Analyze proposals and make recommendations

Instill the importance of ethical conduct by setting an example of ethical behavior to protect information assets. (040603)

Knowledge of:
- Business values and ethical conduct
- Formal business ethics
- Basic and professional human behavior
- Appropriate and legally approved disciplinary actions
- Information privacy laws and security regulations
- Policy development and writing

Skills:
- Execute organizational policies and guidelines
- Coach and mentor
- Develop auditing techniques and processes to monitor conduct

Participate in continuing education, research, networking, and professional organizations to develop, maintain, and advance competencies. (040604)

Knowledge of:
- Professional, academic, and industry resources
- Research techniques
- Components of a best practice RIM program

Skills:
- Identify professional development needs to address gaps
- Identify resources for professional development
- Obtain funding for professional development
- Monitor trends in the profession
- Identify appropriate networking opportunities

Influence the RIM profession by participating in the development of RIM/IG trends, methods, and techniques. (040605)

Knowledge of:
- Local and national RIM profession opportunities
- Industry and business trends relevant to the RIM profession
- Internal and external activities to promote the RIM program

Skills:
- Provide leadership
- Influence RIM peers and organizations
- Promote RIM concepts and knowledge
- Collaborate on professional RIM projects

Empower others through leadership and training to maximize their potential and create a positive work environment. (040606)

Knowledge of:

- Technical and business skills
- Personal strengths and weaknesses
- Career path development
- Training methodologies
- Group and interpersonal dynamics
- Coaching and mentoring techniques

Skills:

- Model RIM values
- Deliver on commitments
- Maintain confidentiality
- Demonstrate honesty and act according to ethical principles
- Apply innovative solutions to make organizational improvements
- Create a work environment that encourages innovation
- Adjust rapidly to new situations warranting attention and resolution
- Lead an inclusive workplace that maximizes everyone's talents to achieve RIM goals
- Seek feedback and opportunities to master new skills
- Identify and define problems that warrant attention and resolution
- Recognize employee achievement
- Exercise good judgment by making sound decisions

Lead teams by coaching, mentoring, and resolving problems to support the business operations of the RIM function. (040607)

Knowledge of:

- Leadership principles, techniques, and methodologies
- Coaching and mentoring techniques
- Problem analysis
- Components of a best practice RIM program
- Conflict resolution techniques

Skills:

- Identify and define the needs for coaching and mentoring
- Identify and define problems that warrant attention and resolution
- Apply techniques to resolve the defined issues
- Plan professional and para-professional development strategies and techniques
- Motivate managers and project teams
- Solve problems
- Mediate to resolve conflict
- Build teams
- Provide leadership and mentoring
- Manage a multi-sector workforce and a variety of work environments

Articulate program goals, recognize individual achievement, and communicate openly with staff. (040608)

Knowledge of:

- Leadership principles, techniques, and methodologies
- Human resource management principles
- Motivational theory and practices
- RIM program goals
- Organizational goals

Skills:

- Communicate appropriately for the task, orally and in writing
- Solicit feedback from staff
- Provide professional and constructive feedback to staff
- Perform appropriate skill assessments
- Align staff with the organization's goals
- Direct and manage all aspects of the RIM program

Foster effectiveness during changes in tasks, work environment, or conditions. (040609)

Knowledge of:

- Organizational change
- Organizational environment and culture
- Organizational policies and procedures
- Conflict management styles and strategies

Skills:

- Adapt behavior and work methods when faced with changes
- Communicate positively
- Cooperate and collaborate during change
- Inspire, motivate, and guide others toward goal accomplishments
- Manage stressful situations
- Handle pressure productively
- Recover quickly from setbacks

Manage and mediate conflict. (040610)

Knowledge of:

- Effects of conflict
- Cross-cultural considerations in dealing with conflict
- Conflict management styles and strategies
- Personality types
- Motivational theories
- Mediation techniques

Skills:

- Assess and manage interpersonal conflict in the RIM profession
- Listen actively to facilitate understanding and prevent conflict
- Demonstrate and identify different courses of action
- Demonstrate honesty and act according to ethical principles
- Foster cooperative working relationships
- Exercise good judgment by making sound decisions
- Negotiate win/win solutions
- Adjust rapidly to new situations that warrant resolution

Facilitate career development by developing individual development plans, instituting reward systems, and providing resources and increased job opportunities. (040611)

Knowledge of:

- Organizational position descriptions and competencies
- Human resource management principles
- Resource availability and requirements
- Organizational staff recognition and promotion methods
- Organizational policies and procedures
- Motivational theory and techniques
- Corporate culture and practical behavior
- Team building and supporting principles and techniques
- RIM profession continuing professional development trends and expectations
- Staff motivation

Skills:

- Develop recognition and reward systems for staff
- Coach and manage staff
- Communicate with staff regarding their individual development plans and performance levels
- Promote the concept of employee ownership and responsibility
- Promote a team-building atmosphere
- Create, endorse, and maintain a diverse workforce
- Map individual development plans to RIM program needs
- Assess and use resources (e.g., training offerings, professional literature) to support staff development requirements

Support opportunities for career development that are consistent with RIM program objectives to improve staff effectiveness. (040612)

Knowledge of:

- Business policies
- Human resource policies
- Management and supervisory principles
- Goal setting
- Performance evaluation methodologies
- Change management
- RIM program strategy and goals
- Business values and ethical conduct

Skills:

- Manage resources and measure performance
- Develop teams and define roles and responsibilities
- Motivate employees
- Facilitate change
- Communicate appropriately for the task, orally and in writing
- Apply conflict resolution tools
- Develop succession plans
- Coach and mentor

Champion the RIM program, establishing its credibility, integrity, and executive presence to heighten organizational awareness of it and position it as a key business resource. (040613)

Knowledge of:

- Strategic value of applying RIM practices to the organization's information assets
- RIM program and how it contributes to best practices
- Regulations and industry guidelines
- Communication techniques
- Business development activity analysis
- Marketing and public relations
- Organizational analysis techniques

Skills:

- Interpret the mission and goals of the organization
- Articulate the goals of the RIM program and how it supports the organization's mission and goals
- Create marketing plans and communication tools
- Manage a changing environment
- Influence stakeholders for RIM support
- Develop partnerships
- Relate RIM goals to the organization's goals

Champion organizational policy and practice to ensure that archival records are secure throughout their life cycle and preserved and managed over time. (040614)

Knowledge of:

- Archives management principles and practices
- RIM program policy and practice for managing historical records and archives
- Archival material preservation principles and practices

Skills:

- Communicate the lasting economic, historical, and informational value of archival records
- Evaluate RIM systems against archival requirements
- Negotiate the preservation of archival materials

Provide direction for creating and implementing a vital records program. (040615)

Knowledge of:

- Core business practices and objectives
- Organizational structure and inter-organizational network
- Industry standards and best practices for vital records programs and management
- Legal and regulatory requirements for information, including privacy requirements for protected information

Skills:

- Validate vital records
- Obtain funding in support of the vital records program
- Assess and prioritize the risks associated with the loss of information assets
- Promote organizational support for a vital records management system
- Document the RIM direction in vital records protection

Provide leadership and strategic direction to capitalize on opportunities for the enterprise-wide RIM program. (040616)

Knowledge of:

- Knowledge management
- Strategic planning
- Enterprise content management
- Customer relationship management
- Financial planning and budgeting
- Business ethics
- Impact on external environments

Skills:

- Analyze RIM program strengths, weaknesses, opportunities, and threats (SWOT)
- Conduct an environmental scan
- Gather and analyze competitive intelligence
- Interpret data into meaningful information
- Adapt to new information or changing conditions

Glossary

This glossary includes a list of acronyms, competency-related terms, records management, and information governance terms commonly used in the competencies document. The sources for each definition not original to this publication is indicated at the end of the definition; most are taken from *Glossary of Records Management and Information Governance Terms*, 5th edition (ARMA International TR 22 – 2016), which is available for purchase at www.arma.org/go/prod/V5032.

ability

The knowledge and skills required for performing successfully at a given level. Competencies are the detailed descriptions of those abilities.

Source: RIM Core Competencies, 2007.

access

The right, opportunity, or means of finding, viewing, using, or retrieving information.

Source: ARMA International Glossary, 5th Ed.

access control

The framework of policy, processes, and tools to control access to a resource or physical facility based on the permission level, role, and responsibilities assigned to the person requesting access.

Source: ARMA International Glossary, 5th Ed.

accession

The process of accepting legal custody and physical control of materials, documenting information about them in a register, database, or log, and establishing parameters for their use.

Source: ARMA International Glossary, 5th Ed.

accountability

The act of holding an individual or organization responsible for a set of activities, requiring them to ensure that the activities meet desired outcomes, and expecting them to explain any variances or non-conformances.

Source: ARMA International Glossary, 5th Ed.

analog record

1. A paper or micrographic record.
2. A record created by a continuously varying quantity, such as photographs and films made with light-sensitive media or sound based on magnetic support.
3. Record copies of audio or video recordings that are not digital.

Source: ARMA International Glossary, 5th Ed.

application program interface (API)

Tools and connectors used by a software program to communicate with the operating system or another software program so data passes seamlessly between programs.

Source: ARMA International Glossary, 5th Ed.

appraisal

The evaluation of a record series or an individual record's value for retention or archival purposes, based upon its current or predicted use(s) for administrative, legal, regulatory, fiscal, research, evidentiary, or historical purposes.

Source: ARMA International Glossary, 5th Ed.

archives

1. The noncurrent records created or received and accumulated by a person or organization in the course of the conduct of affairs and preserved because of their continuing or enduring value.
2. An institution or division within an institution responsible for collecting, organizing, preserving, and providing access to records of enduring value.

Source: ARMA International Glossary, 5th Ed.

audit

A review of information-related activities to ensure that sufficient policies procedures, and controls are in place and complied with to meet all operational, legal, and regulatory obligations and to identify where and how improvements should be made.

Source: ARMA International Glossary, 5th Ed.

authenticity

The sum of the qualities of a record that establishes the origin, reliability, trustworthiness, and correctness of its content.

Source: ARMA International Glossary, 5th Ed.

benchmarking

The act of measuring against specified standards, references, or peer practices.

Source: ARMA International Glossary, 5th Ed.

business continuity plan (BCP)

The documented plan that defines the resources, actions, tasks, and data required to manage the disaster prevention, emergency preparedness, disaster response and recovery, and business resumption process in the event of a business interruption.

Source: ARMA International Glossary, 5th Ed.

catalog

1. A systematically arranged list of records or other items and their descriptive details.
2. The act of creating a descriptive index.

Source: ARMA International Glossary, 5th Ed.

Certified Records Manager (CRM)

A professional records manager who has satisfactorily passed the certified records manager examination administered by the Institute of Certified Records Managers and who remains a member in good standing.

Source: ARMA International Glossary, 5th Ed.

chief information officer (CIO)

The executive with responsibility for managing an organization's information technology and information assets, both strategically and operationally.

Source: ARMA International Glossary, 3rd Ed.

chief records officer (CRO)

A top-level executive officer in an organization and the principal decision maker with responsibility to: ensure that the organization leverages records and information for maximum effectiveness enterprise-wide; direct all aspects of the organization's records and information management program; develop and implement strategies to meet business, legal, and regulatory requirements for records management and compliance; and determine staff levels, equipment, and other resources required to meet the organization's records and information management objectives.

Source: ARMA International Glossary, 5th Ed.

classification system

A system in which related material is filed under a major subject and its subheadings.

Source: ARMA International Glossary, 5th Ed.

competency

Knowledge, skill, characteristic, or trait that contributes to outstanding performance in a particular profession. A competency is represented by a task statement and the associated knowledge and skills required to perform the task.

Source: ARMA International Glossary, 5th Ed.

competency model

A series of competencies organized together. A competency model differentiates between entry level and expert level performance for a specific profession.

Source: ARMA International Glossary, 5th Ed.

compliance

The manner and duties in which an organization conducts its activities in accordance with the requirements of applicable internal and external authorities.

Source: ARMA International Glossary, 5th Ed.

controlled language (vocabulary)

The use of standardized terminology to describe records or other information objects to aid in retrieval.

Source: ARMA International Glossary, 5th Ed.

data

Any symbols or characters that represent raw facts or figures and form the basis of information.

Source: ARMA International Glossary, 5th Ed.

data controller

An entity that has the authority over the processing of personal information. This entity is the focus of most obligations under privacy and data protection laws. It controls the use of personal data by determining the purposes for its use and the manner in which the data will be processed. The data controller may be an individual or an organization that is legally treated as an individual, such as a corporation or partnership.

Source: International Association of Privacy Professionals Certification Textbooks: CIPP/Europe, CIPP/US Government, Foundations.

data processing

Any operation or set of operations which is performed on personal data, such as collecting; recording; organizing; storing; adapting or altering; retrieving; consulting; using; disclosing by transmission, dissemination or otherwise making the data available; aligning or combining data, or blocking, erasing or destroying data. Not limited to automatic means.

Source International Association of Privacy ProfessionalsCertification Textbook F.

de-identification

An action that one takes to remove identifying characteristics from data.

Source: International Association of Privacy Professionals Certification Textbooks: Foundations; CIPP/US Government, CIPT.

destruction hold

A hold placed on the scheduled destruction of records due to foreseeable or pending litigation, governmental investigation, audit or special organizational requirements.

Source: ARMA International Glossary, 5th Ed.

digital
Any data or recorded information that exists as binary codes (zeros and ones).
Source: ARMA International Glossary, 5th Ed.

disaster recovery
Actions the organization will take to restore critical business functions and reclaim damaged or threatened records.
Source: Adapted from definition of "disaster recovery plan" in ARMA International Glossary, 5th Ed.

disposition
For a record, the final action taken per the retention schedule, concluding with destruction, transfer, or permanent preservation.
Source: ARMA International Glossary, 5th Ed.

document:
Information or data fixed in some media, but which is not part of the official record; a nonrecord.
Source: ARMA International Glossary, 5th Ed.

domain
Groups or categories of competencies in a particular performance area that define the major responsibilities or duties that make up the profession. There are six domains used in the Core Competencies: Business Functions, RIM Practices, Risk Management, Communications and Marketing, Information Technology, and Leadership.
Source: ARMA International Glossary, 5th Ed.

duplication
The process of making copies of original documents.
Source: ARMA International Glossary, 5th Ed.

electronic discovery (e-discovery)
Any process by which electronic data is sought, located, secured, preserved, and searched with the intent of using it as evidence in a civil or criminal legal case.

electronic document management system (EDMS)
A system consisting of software, hardware, policies, and processes to automate the preparation, organization, storage, retrieval, tracking, distribution and disposition of electronic documents.
Source: ARMA International Glossary, 5th Ed.

electronic repository
A computer system in which electronic records and their associated metadata are stored.
Source: ARMA International Glossary, 5th Ed.

evidential value
The qualities that are necessary to provide the trustworthiness, reliability, and authenticity of a record and that can be used to prove or disprove a fact in a legal proceeding.
Source: ARMA International Glossary, 5th Ed.

file
A group of documents in any format or media related by subject, activity, or transaction, often handled as a unit. In records management, the file can be electronic, microform, or any other media.
Source: ARMA International Glossary, 5th Ed.

file conversion
The process of changing legacy documents and records from one format, storage media, application, and /or system to another.
Source: ARMA International Glossary, 5th Ed.

Generally Accepted Recordkeeping Principles®

A framework of definitive principles for governing an organization's information as a strategic asset. The information governance principles support organizational goals, facilitate compliance with regulatory, legislative, and information management requirements, and limit risks.
Source: ARMA International Glossary, 5th Ed.

historical value

The determination during appraisal that the item has continuing usefulness or significance in documenting the history of an entity.
Source: ARMA International Glossary, 5th Ed.

information

Data that has been given value through analysis, interpretation, or compilation in a meaningful form.
Source: ARMA International Glossary, 5th Ed.

information architecture (IA)

The structure and interrelationship of information, especially with an eye toward using business rules, observed user behaviors, and effective interface design to facilitate access to the information.
Source: SAA Glossary.

information assets

Data, information, documents, and records may be collectively referred to as information assets.

information technology

See **information systems.**

information systems

The infrastructure, processes, and technologies used to store, generate, manipulate, and transmit information to support an organization.
Source: ARMA International Glossary, 5th Ed.

knowledge

Acquired or learned factual or procedural information that supports the ability to perform a job task.
Source: ARMA International Glossary, 5th Ed.

knowledge management

The strategies and processes designed to identify, capture, structure, value, leverage, and share an organization's intellectual assets to enhance its performance and competitiveness.
Source: ARMA International Glossary, 5th Ed.

legacy data

Information already stored in an old or obsolete format or computer system.

legal hold

See **destruction hold.**

level

A reflection of the amount of knowledge or experience a person has relevant to a specific topic or skill-set—regardless of time in the profession.
Source: ARMA International Glossary, 5th Ed.

life cycle (of a record)

The major milestones of a record's existence, subject to changing requirements creation/receipt, classification, use, retention, and disposition (i.e., transfer to another entity, archival retention, or destruction.)

Source: ARMA International Glossary, 5th Ed.

medium/media

A general term referring to the material onto which business information has been recorded and may subsequently be used.

Source: ARMA International Glossary, 5th Ed.

metadata

Structured information that describes, explains, locates, or otherwise makes it easier to retrieve, use, or manage an information resource.

Source: ARMA International Glossary, 5th Ed.

migration (media)

The process of moving data from one information system or storage medium to another while maintaining the record's authenticity, integrity, reliability, and usability.

Source: ARMA International Glossary, 5th Ed.

model

1. A potential "best practice" representation.
2. The definition of a database describing tables and their interconnections.

Source: ARMA International Glossary, 5th Ed.

objectives

Specific targets established by those involved in their achievement to encourage high performance. Objectives should be unambiguous, results-oriented, measurable, verifiable, relevant, and achievable.

Source: ARMA International Glossary, 5th Ed.

online data storage

Refers to the storage of data by a third-party vendor made accessible through the Internet (Hosted storage, Internet storage, cloud storage). This is a common data storage alternative to local storage, such as on a hard drive, and portable storage, such as a flash drive.

Source: International Association of Privacy Professionals Certification Textbooks

organizational change management

Organizational change management (OCM) is a framework for managing the effect of new business processes, changes in organizational structure or cultural changes within an enterprise. Simply put, OCM addresses the people side of change management.

Source: TechTarget

Payment Card Industry – Data Security Standard (PCI-DSS)

A self-regulatory system that provides an enforceable security standard for payment card data. The rules were drafted by the Payment Card Industry Security Standards Council, which built on previous rules written by the various credit card companies. Except for small companies, compliance with the standard requires hiring a third party to conduct security assessments and detect violations. Failure to comply can lead to exclusion from Visa, MasterCard or other major payment card systems, as well as penalties.

Source: International Association of Privacy Professionals Certification Textbooks: Foundations, CIPM, CIPP/US

personally identifiable information (PII)
Any information that can be used in isolation or in combination with other sources to uniquely identify, contact, or locate a specific individual.
Source: ARMA International Glossary, 5th Ed.

policy
A high-level overall plan, containing a set of principles, embracing the general goals of the organization, and used to base decisions.
Source: RIM Core Competencies, 2007.

preservation
Process and operation involved in ensuring the technical and intellectual survival of authentic records through time.
Source: ARMA International Glossary, 5th Ed.

privacy breach response
The IAPP response guidelines for organizations to follow when their system for protecting individual privacy has experienced a failure.
Source: ARMA International Glossary, 5th Ed.

Privacy Impact Assessment (PIA)
An analysis of how information is handled (i) to ensure handling conforms to applicable legal, regulatory and policy requirements regarding privacy; (ii) to determine the risks and effects of collecting, maintaining and disseminating information in identifiable form in an electronic information system, and (iii) to examine and evaluate protections and alternative processes for handling information to mitigate potential privacy risks
Source: RIM Core Competencies, 2007.

privacy policy
An internal statement that governs an organization or entity's handling practices of personal information. It is directed at the users of the personal information. A privacy policy instructs employees on the collection and the use of the data, as well as any specific rights the data subjects may have.
Source: International Association of Privacy ProfessionalsCertification Textbooks: Foundations, CIPP/US Government, CIPP/US.

privacy review
An analysis of all new projects for their compliance with the privacy standard and privacy policy of an organization. Reviews should be performed multiple times beginning at the early stages of new project development to minimize potential privacy risks.
Source: International Association of Privacy Professionals Certification Textbook: CIPT.

privacy standard
The minimum level at which privacy should be protected in all new projects, applications and services. This includes the expectations of privacy in the new programs and guidelines for adherence to those standards. The standard is set based on both internal organizational policy and external regulations etc.
Source: International Association of Privacy Professionals Certification Textbook: CIPT.

procedure
Instructions, exhibits, and/or other methodologies to follow in order to complete tasks in a predictable and orderly way.
Source: ARMA International Glossary, 5th Ed.

protected health information (PHI)

Any individually identifiable health information transmitted or maintained in any form or medium that is held by a covered entity or its business associate; identifies the individual or offers a reasonable basis for identification; is created or received by a covered entity or an employer, and relates to a past, present or future physical or mental condition, provision of healthcare or payment for healthcare to that individual.

Source: International Association of Privacy Professionals Certification Textbook: CIPM, CIPP/US, CIPP/US Government.

protected information*

Any readable information that can be linked to a specific individual.

See also: protected health information (PHI), personally identifiable information (PII), sensitive personally identifiable information (SPII), and payment card industry data security standard (PCI-DSS).

Source: ARMA International Glossary, 5th Ed.

radio frequency identification (RFID)

Technology that uses radio frequencies and a data tag to identify, track, locate, and manage items.

Source: ARMA International Glossary, 5th Ed.

record

Any recorded information, regardless of medium or characteristics, made or received and retained by an organization in pursuance of legal obligations or in the transaction of business.

Source: ARMA International Glossary, 5th Ed.

records appraisal

See **appraisal.**

records center

1. (digital records) A storage device with lower operating costs, which may be online or offline depending on the speed and frequency of access required for the records.
2. (paper records) An area for lower-cost storage, maintenance, and reference use of semiactive records pending their ultimate disposition.

Source: ARMA International Glossary, 5th Ed.

records and information management (RIM)

The field of management responsible for establishing and implementing policies, systems, and procedures to capture, create, access, distribute, use, store, secure, retrieve, and ensure disposition of an organization's records and information. **records inventory**

A detailed listing that includes the types, locations, dates, volumes, equipment, classification systems, and usage data of an organization's records

Source: ARMA International Glossary, 5th Ed.

records series

A group of related records filed/used together as a unit and evaluated as a unit for retention purposes, e.g., a personnel file consisting or an application, reference letters, benefit forms, etc.

Source: ARMA International Glossary, 5th Ed.

records retention schedule

A comprehensive list of records series, indicating for each the length of time it is to be maintained. Also referred to as *retention schedule* or *records schedule.*

Source: ARMA International Glossary, 5th Ed.

redaction

The process of masking or removing sensitive information in a document before releasing it for public use.
Source: ARMA International Glossary, 5th Ed.

return on investment (ROI)

A cost justification method for an investment (e.g., purchase of hardware or software) that compares the cost outflows (expenses) to the cash inflows (benefits.).
Source: ARMA International Glossary, 5th Ed.

risk assessment

The evaluation of the possibility of incurring loss, damage, or injury and a determination of the amount of risk that is acceptable for a given situation or event.
Source: ARMA International Glossary, 5th Ed.

risk management

The identification, assessment, and prioritization of risks (defined as the effect of uncertainty on objectives, whether positive or negative) followed by coordinated and economical application of resources to minimize, monitor, and control the probability and/or impact of undesired events.
Source: ARMA International Glossary, 5th Ed.

schema

1. A set of rules or a conceptual model for data structure and content, such as a description of the data content and relationships in a database. *Source:* ARMA International Glossary, 5th Ed.

2. In XML, a language used to express the constraints of an XML document *Source: RIM Core Competencies,* 2007

3. Logical plan showing the relationship between metadata elements, normally through establishing rules for the use and management of metadata specifically as regards the semantics, the syntax and optionality (obligation level) of values.
Source: ISO 23081-1

security classification

A classification placed on records limiting their accessibility for retrieval or use.
Source: ARMA International Glossary, 5th Ed.

sensitive personally identifiable information (SPII)

Personally Identifiable Information, which if lost, compromised, or disclosed without authorization, could result in substantial harm, embarrassment, inconvenience, or unfairness to an individual.
Source: Handbook for Safeguarding Sensitive PII

skill

The observable, quantifiable, and measurable performance parameters involving physical, verbal, or mental manipulation of data, people, or objects.
Source: RIM Core Competencies, 2007

stakeholder

Individual in leadership positions within an organization who lead and own disciplines related to records management, including but not limited to executives (e.g., the Board of Directors), privacy, security, internal audit, general counsel, and the business/operations.
Source: International Association of Privacy Professionals Certification Textbook: CIPM.

standard

A method, material, or practice developed through consensus by experts in the field, which leads to results that are consistent, predictable, and desirable.

Source: ARMA International Glossary, 5th Ed.

SWOT analysis

A particular method for presenting information in the form of an assessment of strengths, weaknesses, opportunities, and threats that serves as an aid to decision-making.

Source: ARMA International Glossary, 5th Ed.

task

A specific work activity required for a job at the defined level and domain

Source: ARMA International Glossary, 5th Ed.

taxonomy

A collection of controlled vocabulary terms used to describe an organization's information components. The taxonomy may or may not be organized in a hierarchical structure.

Source: ARMA International Glossary, 5th Ed.

tracking

The component of a records management system that ensures records can be located when needed.

Source: ARMA International Glossary, 5th Ed.

value

The usefulness, significance, or worth of a record.

Source: ARMA International Glossary, 5th Ed.

version

One of two or more iterations in which a document has been modified and is different in some way from another form of the same document.

Source: ARMA International Glossary, 5th Ed.

vital record

A record that is fundamental to the functioning of an organization and necessary to the continuance of operations.

Source: ARMA International Glossary, 5th Ed.

workflow

1. A series of tasks defined within an organization to produce a final outcome.
2. The technology of implementing business processes as a controlled and conditional sequence of steps, ad hoc or business rule-based, each having tasks to be performed by users or other applications where information has to be analyzed and new information is fed into the system.

Source: ARMA International Glossary, 5th Ed.

Bibliography

ARMA International. *Glossary of Records Management Terms*, 3rd Ed. Lenexa, KS: ARMA International, 2007.

_____. *Glossary of Records Management and Information Governance Terms*, 5th Ed. (ARMA International 22-2016). Overland Park, KS: ARMA International, 2016.

_____. *Records and Information Management Core Competencies*. Lenexa, KS: ARMA International, 2007.

International Association of Privacy Professionals Certification Textbooks. Portsmouth, NH:

      C: CIPP/Canada

      E: CIPP/Europe

      F: Foundations

      G: CIPP/US Government T: CIPT

      M: CIPM

      U: CIPP/US

_____. "Glossary of Privacy Terms." Available at *https://iapp.org/resources/glossary/*.

International Organization for Standardization. *Information and documentation – Records management – Part 1: Concepts and principles, 2016*, ISO 15489: 2016. Geneva, Switzerland: International Organization for Standardization, 2006.

_____. *Information and documentation – Records management processes – Metadata for records – Part 1: Principles*, ISO 23081-1: 2006. Geneva, Switzerland: International Organization for Standardization, 2006.

_____. *Information and documentation – Records management processes – Metadata for records – Part 2: Conceptual and implementation issues*, ISO 23081-2: 2009. Geneva, Switzerland: International Organization for Standardization, 2009.

_____. *Information and documentation – Records management processes – Metadata for records – Part 3: Self-Assessment Method*, ISO 23081-3: 2011. Geneva, Switzerland: International Organization for Standardization, 2011.

National Archives of the United Kingdom. "What is an information asset?" Available at *www.nationalarchives.gov.uk/documents/information-management/information-assets-factsh*.

Sedona Conference®, The. *The Sedona Conference® 2010 Commentary on Legal Holds: The Trigger & The Process*. Sedona, AZ: The Sedona Conference®, 2010.

Society of American Archivists. *Glossary of Archival and Records Terminology*. Chicago: Society of American Archivists, 2005.

TechTarget. Glossary. Available at *http://searchcio.techtarget.com/definition/organizational-change-management-OCM*.

2007 RIM Core Competencies Development Project

The original ARMA International *Records and Information Management Core Competencies* publication was developed by the Core Competencies Working Group established by ARMA's Education Development Committee (EDC). The EDC enlisted many experienced records and information management (RIM) professionals to bring the core competencies to life. The initial two-year development process included the input of a 15-member writing team, 40 RIM subject matter experts who created the initial draft, and 300 subject matter experts who completed a validation survey and reviewed, edited, and commented on the core competencies.

2007 RIM Core Competencies Writing Team Members

Jacki Conn, ARMA International

Raymond K. Cunningham, Jr., CRM, CA, CIPP, University of Illinois Foundation

Carol Choksy, PhD, CRM, PMP, IRAD Strategic Consulting, Inc.

Kathleen Dedig, CRM, OGE Energy Corp.

Richard Head, ARMA International

Kevin Joerling, CRM, ARMA International

William LeFevre, CA, CRM, Wayne State University

Deborah J. Marshall, LECG

Susan McKinney, CRM, University of Minnesota

Lawrence Medina, Lawrence Livermore National Laboratory

Mike Miller, Ph.D., CRM, CA, Lockheed Martin

William Millican, ARMA International

Cheryl Pederson, CRM, Cargill Inc.

Roberta Shaffer – *EDC Chair,* Library of Congress

David B. Steward, CRM, Blackwell Sanders LLP

2007 RIM Job Task Analysis Meeting Participants

Christine Ardern, CRM, FAI

Belinda Bartels, CRM

Jayne Bellyk, CRM

Marilyn Bier

Sharon Burnett

Diane Carlisle, CRM

Beth Chiaiese, CRM

Jacki Conn

Margaret Crockett

Raymond K. Cunningham, Jr., CRM, CA, CIPP

Keith Davis

Evelyn Farrell

Leatrice Garcia

Debra Gearhart, CRM, FAI

Janet Johnson, CRM

Cynthia Kent, CRM

Nancy Kunde, CRM, CA

Paula Johnson

Gary Lewis, CRM, CDIA+

Lori Ann Lindberg

William F. Lynch III

Robert Marraro

Deborah J. Marshall

Kristina McConnell

Brenda McCoy-Manfredo

David McDermott, CRM

Susan McKinney, CRM

Lawrence Medina

Mike Miller, Ph.D., CRM, CA

William Millican

Diana Newman

Linda Pace

Cheryl Pederson, CRM

Blake Richardson, CRM

Suzanne Sawyer

Roberta Shaffer, J.D.

Preston Shimer, FAI

John Smith, CRM, CBCP

Thomas Smith, CRM, CCP

Leslie Strange

Helen Streck

Sarah Earlene Swindall, CRM

Thomas Daniel Walters

Richard Weinholdt

Mary White Dollman, CRM

Jesse Wilkins, CDIA+

Richard Wilson

About ARMA International

ARMA International is a not-for-profit professional association and the authority on governing information as a strategic asset. Established in 1955, the association's approximate 27,000+ members include information governance professionals, archivists, corporate librarians, imaging specialists, legal professionals, IT managers, consultants, and educators, all of whom work in a variety of industries, including government, legal, healthcare, financial services, and petroleum in the United States, Canada, and more than 30 countries around the globe.

ARMA International's mission is to provide informational professionals the resources, tools, and training they need to effectively manage records and information within an established information governance framework.

The ARMA International headquarters office is in Overland Park, Kansas, in the Kansas City metropolitan area. Office hours are 8:30 a.m. to 5:00 p.m. (CT), Monday through Friday.

ARMA International
11880 College Blvd., Suite 450
Overland Park, KS 66210913.341.3808
Fax: 913.341.3742
headquarters@armaintl.org
www.arma.org

Made in the USA
Middletown, DE
31 May 2021